MW01108029

This Journal Belongs to:

_____

Weather Journal

Date		Sunrise		Sunset	
Sunny	Partly Cloudy	Cloudy	Wind Speed		
Temp Hi	Lo	Humidity		Dewpoint	
Barometric Pressure		Precipitation Amount			
Rain	Sleet	Freezing Rain	Snow	Snow Depth	

Date		Sunrise		Sunset	
Sunny	Partly Cloudy	Cloudy	Wind Speed		
Temp Hi	Lo	Humidity		Dewpoint	
Barometric Pressure		Precipitation Amount			
Rain	Sleet	Freezing Rain	Snow	Snow Depth	

Date		Sunrise		Sunset	
Sunny	Partly Cloudy	Cloudy	Wind Speed		
Temp Hi	Lo	Humidity		Dewpoint	
Barometric Pressure		Precipitation Amount			
Rain	Sleet	Freezing Rain	Snow	Snow Depth	

Weather Journal

Date		Sunrise		Sunset	
Sunny	Partly Cloudy	Cloudy	Wind Speed		
Temp Hi Lo		Humidity		Dewpoint	
Barometric Pressure		Precipitation Amount			
Rain	Sleet	Freezing Rain	Snow	Snow Depth	

Date		Sunrise		Sunset	
Sunny	Partly Cloudy	Cloudy	Wind Speed		
Temp Hi Lo		Humidity		Dewpoint	
Barometric Pressure		Precipitation Amount			
Rain	Sleet	Freezing Rain	Snow	Snow Depth	

Date		Sunrise		Sunset	
Sunny	Partly Cloudy	Cloudy	Wind Speed		
Temp Hi Lo		Humidity		Dewpoint	
Barometric Pressure		Precipitation Amount			
Rain	Sleet	Freezing Rain	Snow	Snow Depth	

Weather Journal

Date			Sunrise		Sunset	
Sunny	Partly Cloudy		Cloudy	Wind Speed		
Temp Hi Lo			Humidity		Dewpoint	
Barometric Pressure			Precipitation Amount			
Rain	Sleet		Freezing Rain	Snow	Snow Depth	

Date			Sunrise		Sunset	
Sunny	Partly Cloudy		Cloudy	Wind Speed		
Temp Hi Lo			Humidity		Dewpoint	
Barometric Pressure			Precipitation Amount			
Rain	Sleet		Freezing Rain	Snow	Snow Depth	

Date			Sunrise		Sunset	
Sunny	Partly Cloudy		Cloudy	Wind Speed		
Temp Hi Lo			Humidity		Dewpoint	
Barometric Pressure			Precipitation Amount			
Rain	Sleet		Freezing Rain	Snow	Snow Depth	

Weather Journal

Date		Sunrise		Sunset	
Sunny	Partly Cloudy	Cloudy	Wind Speed		
Temp Hi	Lo	Humidity		Dewpoint	
Barometric Pressure		Precipitation Amount			
Rain	Sleet	Freezing Rain	Snow	Snow Depth	

Date		Sunrise		Sunset	
Sunny	Partly Cloudy	Cloudy	Wind Speed		
Temp Hi	Lo	Humidity		Dewpoint	
Barometric Pressure		Precipitation Amount			
Rain	Sleet	Freezing Rain	Snow	Snow Depth	

Date		Sunrise		Sunset	
Sunny	Partly Cloudy	Cloudy	Wind Speed		
Temp Hi	Lo	Humidity		Dewpoint	
Barometric Pressure		Precipitation Amount			
Rain	Sleet	Freezing Rain	Snow	Snow Depth	

Weather Journal

Date		Sunrise		Sunset	
Sunny	Partly Cloudy	Cloudy	Wind Speed		
Temp Hi	Lo	Humidity		Dewpoint	
Barometric Pressure		Precipitation Amount			
Rain	Sleet	Freezing Rain	Snow	Snow Depth	

Date		Sunrise		Sunset	
Sunny	Partly Cloudy	Cloudy	Wind Speed		
Temp Hi	Lo	Humidity		Dewpoint	
Barometric Pressure		Precipitation Amount			
Rain	Sleet	Freezing Rain	Snow	Snow Depth	

Date		Sunrise		Sunset	
Sunny	Partly Cloudy	Cloudy	Wind Speed		
Temp Hi	Lo	Humidity		Dewpoint	
Barometric Pressure		Precipitation Amount			
Rain	Sleet	Freezing Rain	Snow	Snow Depth	

Weather Journal

Date		Sunrise		Sunset	
Sunny	Partly Cloudy	Cloudy	Wind Speed		
Temp Hi	Lo	Humidity		Dewpoint	
Barometric Pressure		Precipitation Amount			
Rain	Sleet	Freezing Rain	Snow	Snow Depth	

Date		Sunrise		Sunset	
Sunny	Partly Cloudy	Cloudy	Wind Speed		
Temp Hi	Lo	Humidity		Dewpoint	
Barometric Pressure		Precipitation Amount			
Rain	Sleet	Freezing Rain	Snow	Snow Depth	

Date		Sunrise		Sunset	
Sunny	Partly Cloudy	Cloudy	Wind Speed		
Temp Hi	Lo	Humidity		Dewpoint	
Barometric Pressure		Precipitation Amount			
Rain	Sleet	Freezing Rain	Snow	Snow Depth	

Weather Journal

Date		Sunrise		Sunset	
Sunny	Partly Cloudy	Cloudy	Wind Speed		
Temp Hi	Lo	Humidity		Dewpoint	
Barometric Pressure		Precipitation Amount			
Rain	Sleet	Freezing Rain	Snow	Snow Depth	

Date		Sunrise		Sunset	
Sunny	Partly Cloudy	Cloudy	Wind Speed		
Temp Hi	Lo	Humidity		Dewpoint	
Barometric Pressure		Precipitation Amount			
Rain	Sleet	Freezing Rain	Snow	Snow Depth	

Date		Sunrise		Sunset	
Sunny	Partly Cloudy	Cloudy	Wind Speed		
Temp Hi	Lo	Humidity		Dewpoint	
Barometric Pressure		Precipitation Amount			
Rain	Sleet	Freezing Rain	Snow	Snow Depth	

Weather Journal

Date		Sunrise		Sunset	
Sunny	Partly Cloudy	Cloudy	Wind Speed		
Temp Hi	Lo	Humidity		Dewpoint	
Barometric Pressure		Precipitation Amount			
Rain	Sleet	Freezing Rain	Snow	Snow Depth	

Date		Sunrise		Sunset	
Sunny	Partly Cloudy	Cloudy	Wind Speed		
Temp Hi	Lo	Humidity		Dewpoint	
Barometric Pressure		Precipitation Amount			
Rain	Sleet	Freezing Rain	Snow	Snow Depth	

Date		Sunrise		Sunset	
Sunny	Partly Cloudy	Cloudy	Wind Speed		
Temp Hi	Lo	Humidity		Dewpoint	
Barometric Pressure		Precipitation Amount			
Rain	Sleet	Freezing Rain	Snow	Snow Depth	

Weather Journal

Date			Sunrise		Sunset	
Sunny	Partly Cloudy		Cloudy	Wind Speed		
Temp Hi	Lo		Humidity		Dewpoint	
Barometric Pressure			Precipitation Amount			
Rain	Sleet		Freezing Rain	Snow	Snow Depth	

Date			Sunrise		Sunset	
Sunny	Partly Cloudy		Cloudy	Wind Speed		
Temp Hi	Lo		Humidity		Dewpoint	
Barometric Pressure			Precipitation Amount			
Rain	Sleet		Freezing Rain	Snow	Snow Depth	

Date			Sunrise		Sunset	
Sunny	Partly Cloudy		Cloudy	Wind Speed		
Temp Hi	Lo		Humidity		Dewpoint	
Barometric Pressure			Precipitation Amount			
Rain	Sleet		Freezing Rain	Snow	Snow Depth	

Weather Journal

Date		Sunrise		Sunset	
Sunny	Partly Cloudy	Cloudy	Wind Speed		
Temp Hi	Lo	Humidity		Dewpoint	
Barometric Pressure		Precipitation Amount			
Rain	Sleet	Freezing Rain	Snow	Snow Depth	

Date		Sunrise		Sunset	
Sunny	Partly Cloudy	Cloudy	Wind Speed		
Temp Hi	Lo	Humidity		Dewpoint	
Barometric Pressure		Precipitation Amount			
Rain	Sleet	Freezing Rain	Snow	Snow Depth	

Date		Sunrise		Sunset	
Sunny	Partly Cloudy	Cloudy	Wind Speed		
Temp Hi	Lo	Humidity		Dewpoint	
Barometric Pressure		Precipitation Amount			
Rain	Sleet	Freezing Rain	Snow	Snow Depth	

Weather Journal

Date		Sunrise		Sunset	
Sunny	Partly Cloudy	Cloudy	Wind Speed		
Temp Hi	Lo	Humidity		Dewpoint	
Barometric Pressure		Precipitation Amount			
Rain	Sleet	Freezing Rain	Snow	Snow Depth	

Date		Sunrise		Sunset	
Sunny	Partly Cloudy	Cloudy	Wind Speed		
Temp Hi	Lo	Humidity		Dewpoint	
Barometric Pressure		Precipitation Amount			
Rain	Sleet	Freezing Rain	Snow	Snow Depth	

Date		Sunrise		Sunset	
Sunny	Partly Cloudy	Cloudy	Wind Speed		
Temp Hi	Lo	Humidity		Dewpoint	
Barometric Pressure		Precipitation Amount			
Rain	Sleet	Freezing Rain	Snow	Snow Depth	

Weather Journal

Date			Sunrise		Sunset	
Sunny	Partly Cloudy		Cloudy	Wind Speed		
Temp Hi	Lo		Humidity		Dewpoint	
Barometric Pressure			Precipitation Amount			
Rain	Sleet		Freezing Rain	Snow	Snow Depth	

Date			Sunrise		Sunset	
Sunny	Partly Cloudy		Cloudy	Wind Speed		
Temp Hi	Lo		Humidity		Dewpoint	
Barometric Pressure			Precipitation Amount			
Rain	Sleet		Freezing Rain	Snow	Snow Depth	

Date			Sunrise		Sunset	
Sunny	Partly Cloudy		Cloudy	Wind Speed		
Temp Hi	Lo		Humidity		Dewpoint	
Barometric Pressure			Precipitation Amount			
Rain	Sleet		Freezing Rain	Snow	Snow Depth	

Weather Journal

Date		Sunrise		Sunset	
Sunny	Partly Cloudy	Cloudy	Wind Speed		
Temp Hi Lo		Humidity		Dewpoint	
Barometric Pressure		Precipitation Amount			
Rain	Sleet	Freezing Rain	Snow	Snow Depth	

Date		Sunrise		Sunset	
Sunny	Partly Cloudy	Cloudy	Wind Speed		
Temp Hi Lo		Humidity		Dewpoint	
Barometric Pressure		Precipitation Amount			
Rain	Sleet	Freezing Rain	Snow	Snow Depth	

Date		Sunrise		Sunset	
Sunny	Partly Cloudy	Cloudy	Wind Speed		
Temp Hi Lo		Humidity		Dewpoint	
Barometric Pressure		Precipitation Amount			
Rain	Sleet	Freezing Rain	Snow	Snow Depth	

Weather Journal

Date		Sunrise		Sunset	
Sunny	Partly Cloudy	Cloudy	Wind Speed		
Temp Hi Lo		Humidity		Dewpoint	
Barometric Pressure		Precipitation Amount			
Rain	Sleet	Freezing Rain	Snow	Snow Depth	

Date		Sunrise		Sunset	
Sunny	Partly Cloudy	Cloudy	Wind Speed		
Temp Hi Lo		Humidity		Dewpoint	
Barometric Pressure		Precipitation Amount			
Rain	Sleet	Freezing Rain	Snow	Snow Depth	

Date		Sunrise		Sunset	
Sunny	Partly Cloudy	Cloudy	Wind Speed		
Temp Hi Lo		Humidity		Dewpoint	
Barometric Pressure		Precipitation Amount			
Rain	Sleet	Freezing Rain	Snow	Snow Depth	

Weather Journal

Date		Sunrise		Sunset	
Sunny	Partly Cloudy	Cloudy	Wind Speed		
Temp Hi Lo		Humidity		Dewpoint	
Barometric Pressure		Precipitation Amount			
Rain	Sleet	Freezing Rain	Snow	Snow Depth	

Date		Sunrise		Sunset	
Sunny	Partly Cloudy	Cloudy	Wind Speed		
Temp Hi Lo		Humidity		Dewpoint	
Barometric Pressure		Precipitation Amount			
Rain	Sleet	Freezing Rain	Snow	Snow Depth	

Date		Sunrise		Sunset	
Sunny	Partly Cloudy	Cloudy	Wind Speed		
Temp Hi Lo		Humidity		Dewpoint	
Barometric Pressure		Precipitation Amount			
Rain	Sleet	Freezing Rain	Snow	Snow Depth	

Weather Journal

Date		Sunrise		Sunset	
Sunny	Partly Cloudy	Cloudy		Wind Speed	
Temp Hi	Lo	Humidity		Dewpoint	
Barometric Pressure		Precipitation Amount			
Rain	Sleet	Freezing Rain	Snow	Snow Depth	

Date		Sunrise		Sunset	
Sunny	Partly Cloudy	Cloudy		Wind Speed	
Temp Hi	Lo	Humidity		Dewpoint	
Barometric Pressure		Precipitation Amount			
Rain	Sleet	Freezing Rain	Snow	Snow Depth	

Date		Sunrise		Sunset	
Sunny	Partly Cloudy	Cloudy		Wind Speed	
Temp Hi	Lo	Humidity		Dewpoint	
Barometric Pressure		Precipitation Amount			
Rain	Sleet	Freezing Rain	Snow	Snow Depth	

Weather Journal

Date		Sunrise		Sunset	
Sunny	Partly Cloudy	Cloudy	Wind Speed		
Temp Hi	Lo	Humidity		Dewpoint	
Barometric Pressure		Precipitation Amount			
Rain	Sleet	Freezing Rain	Snow	Snow Depth	

Date		Sunrise		Sunset	
Sunny	Partly Cloudy	Cloudy	Wind Speed		
Temp Hi	Lo	Humidity		Dewpoint	
Barometric Pressure		Precipitation Amount			
Rain	Sleet	Freezing Rain	Snow	Snow Depth	

Date		Sunrise		Sunset	
Sunny	Partly Cloudy	Cloudy	Wind Speed		
Temp Hi	Lo	Humidity		Dewpoint	
Barometric Pressure		Precipitation Amount			
Rain	Sleet	Freezing Rain	Snow	Snow Depth	

Weather Journal

Date		Sunrise		Sunset	
Sunny	Partly Cloudy	Cloudy	Wind Speed		
Temp Hi	Lo	Humidity		Dewpoint	
Barometric Pressure		Precipitation Amount			
Rain	Sleet	Freezing Rain	Snow	Snow Depth	

Date		Sunrise		Sunset	
Sunny	Partly Cloudy	Cloudy	Wind Speed		
Temp Hi	Lo	Humidity		Dewpoint	
Barometric Pressure		Precipitation Amount			
Rain	Sleet	Freezing Rain	Snow	Snow Depth	

Date		Sunrise		Sunset	
Sunny	Partly Cloudy	Cloudy	Wind Speed		
Temp Hi	Lo	Humidity		Dewpoint	
Barometric Pressure		Precipitation Amount			
Rain	Sleet	Freezing Rain	Snow	Snow Depth	

Weather Journal

Date		Sunrise		Sunset	
Sunny	Partly Cloudy	Cloudy	Wind Speed		
Temp Hi Lo		Humidity		Dewpoint	
Barometric Pressure		Precipitation Amount			
Rain	Sleet	Freezing Rain	Snow	Snow Depth	

Date		Sunrise		Sunset	
Sunny	Partly Cloudy	Cloudy	Wind Speed		
Temp Hi Lo		Humidity		Dewpoint	
Barometric Pressure		Precipitation Amount			
Rain	Sleet	Freezing Rain	Snow	Snow Depth	

Date		Sunrise		Sunset	
Sunny	Partly Cloudy	Cloudy	Wind Speed		
Temp Hi Lo		Humidity		Dewpoint	
Barometric Pressure		Precipitation Amount			
Rain	Sleet	Freezing Rain	Snow	Snow Depth	

Weather Journal

Date		Sunrise		Sunset	
Sunny	Partly Cloudy	Cloudy	Wind Speed		
Temp Hi	Lo	Humidity		Dewpoint	
Barometric Pressure		Precipitation Amount			
Rain	Sleet	Freezing Rain	Snow	Snow Depth	

Date		Sunrise		Sunset	
Sunny	Partly Cloudy	Cloudy	Wind Speed		
Temp Hi	Lo	Humidity		Dewpoint	
Barometric Pressure		Precipitation Amount			
Rain	Sleet	Freezing Rain	Snow	Snow Depth	

Date		Sunrise		Sunset	
Sunny	Partly Cloudy	Cloudy	Wind Speed		
Temp Hi	Lo	Humidity		Dewpoint	
Barometric Pressure		Precipitation Amount			
Rain	Sleet	Freezing Rain	Snow	Snow Depth	

Weather Journal

Date		Sunrise		Sunset	
Sunny	Partly Cloudy	Cloudy	Wind Speed		
Temp Hi	Lo	Humidity		Dewpoint	
Barometric Pressure		Precipitation Amount			
Rain	Sleet	Freezing Rain	Snow	Snow Depth	

Date		Sunrise		Sunset	
Sunny	Partly Cloudy	Cloudy	Wind Speed		
Temp Hi	Lo	Humidity		Dewpoint	
Barometric Pressure		Precipitation Amount			
Rain	Sleet	Freezing Rain	Snow	Snow Depth	

Date		Sunrise		Sunset	
Sunny	Partly Cloudy	Cloudy	Wind Speed		
Temp Hi	Lo	Humidity		Dewpoint	
Barometric Pressure		Precipitation Amount			
Rain	Sleet	Freezing Rain	Snow	Snow Depth	

Weather Journal

Date		Sunrise		Sunset	
Sunny	Partly Cloudy	Cloudy	Wind Speed		
Temp Hi	Lo	Humidity		Dewpoint	
Barometric Pressure		Precipitation Amount			
Rain	Sleet	Freezing Rain	Snow	Snow Depth	

Date		Sunrise		Sunset	
Sunny	Partly Cloudy	Cloudy	Wind Speed		
Temp Hi	Lo	Humidity		Dewpoint	
Barometric Pressure		Precipitation Amount			
Rain	Sleet	Freezing Rain	Snow	Snow Depth	

Date		Sunrise		Sunset	
Sunny	Partly Cloudy	Cloudy	Wind Speed		
Temp Hi	Lo	Humidity		Dewpoint	
Barometric Pressure		Precipitation Amount			
Rain	Sleet	Freezing Rain	Snow	Snow Depth	

Weather Journal

Date		Sunrise		Sunset	
Sunny	Partly Cloudy	Cloudy		Wind Speed	
Temp Hi Lo		Humidity		Dewpoint	
Barometric Pressure		Precipitation Amount			
Rain	Sleet	Freezing Rain	Snow	Snow Depth	

Date		Sunrise		Sunset	
Sunny	Partly Cloudy	Cloudy		Wind Speed	
Temp Hi Lo		Humidity		Dewpoint	
Barometric Pressure		Precipitation Amount			
Rain	Sleet	Freezing Rain	Snow	Snow Depth	

Date		Sunrise		Sunset	
Sunny	Partly Cloudy	Cloudy		Wind Speed	
Temp Hi Lo		Humidity		Dewpoint	
Barometric Pressure		Precipitation Amount			
Rain	Sleet	Freezing Rain	Snow	Snow Depth	

Weather Journal

Date		Sunrise		Sunset	
Sunny	Partly Cloudy	Cloudy	Wind Speed		
Temp Hi	Lo	Humidity		Dewpoint	
Barometric Pressure		Precipitation Amount			
Rain	Sleet	Freezing Rain	Snow	Snow Depth	

Date		Sunrise		Sunset	
Sunny	Partly Cloudy	Cloudy	Wind Speed		
Temp Hi	Lo	Humidity		Dewpoint	
Barometric Pressure		Precipitation Amount			
Rain	Sleet	Freezing Rain	Snow	Snow Depth	

Date		Sunrise		Sunset	
Sunny	Partly Cloudy	Cloudy	Wind Speed		
Temp Hi	Lo	Humidity		Dewpoint	
Barometric Pressure		Precipitation Amount			
Rain	Sleet	Freezing Rain	Snow	Snow Depth	

Weather Journal

Date		Sunrise		Sunset	
Sunny	Partly Cloudy	Cloudy	Wind Speed		
Temp Hi Lo		Humidity		Dewpoint	
Barometric Pressure		Precipitation Amount			
Rain	Sleet	Freezing Rain	Snow	Snow Depth	

Date		Sunrise		Sunset	
Sunny	Partly Cloudy	Cloudy	Wind Speed		
Temp Hi Lo		Humidity		Dewpoint	
Barometric Pressure		Precipitation Amount			
Rain	Sleet	Freezing Rain	Snow	Snow Depth	

Date		Sunrise		Sunset	
Sunny	Partly Cloudy	Cloudy	Wind Speed		
Temp Hi Lo		Humidity		Dewpoint	
Barometric Pressure		Precipitation Amount			
Rain	Sleet	Freezing Rain	Snow	Snow Depth	

Weather Journal

Date		Sunrise		Sunset	
Sunny	Partly Cloudy	Cloudy	Wind Speed		
Temp Hi	Lo	Humidity		Dewpoint	
Barometric Pressure		Precipitation Amount			
Rain	Sleet	Freezing Rain	Snow	Snow Depth	

Date		Sunrise		Sunset	
Sunny	Partly Cloudy	Cloudy	Wind Speed		
Temp Hi	Lo	Humidity		Dewpoint	
Barometric Pressure		Precipitation Amount			
Rain	Sleet	Freezing Rain	Snow	Snow Depth	

Date		Sunrise		Sunset	
Sunny	Partly Cloudy	Cloudy	Wind Speed		
Temp Hi	Lo	Humidity		Dewpoint	
Barometric Pressure		Precipitation Amount			
Rain	Sleet	Freezing Rain	Snow	Snow Depth	

Weather Journal

Date		Sunrise		Sunset	
Sunny	Partly Cloudy	Cloudy	Wind Speed		
Temp Hi Lo		Humidity		Dewpoint	
Barometric Pressure		Precipitation Amount			
Rain	Sleet	Freezing Rain	Snow	Snow Depth	

Date		Sunrise		Sunset	
Sunny	Partly Cloudy	Cloudy	Wind Speed		
Temp Hi Lo		Humidity		Dewpoint	
Barometric Pressure		Precipitation Amount			
Rain	Sleet	Freezing Rain	Snow	Snow Depth	

Date		Sunrise		Sunset	
Sunny	Partly Cloudy	Cloudy	Wind Speed		
Temp Hi Lo		Humidity		Dewpoint	
Barometric Pressure		Precipitation Amount			
Rain	Sleet	Freezing Rain	Snow	Snow Depth	

Weather Journal

Date			Sunrise		Sunset	
Sunny	Partly Cloudy		Cloudy	Wind Speed		
Temp Hi	Lo		Humidity		Dewpoint	
Barometric Pressure			Precipitation Amount			
Rain	Sleet		Freezing Rain	Snow	Snow Depth	

Date			Sunrise		Sunset	
Sunny	Partly Cloudy		Cloudy	Wind Speed		
Temp Hi	Lo		Humidity		Dewpoint	
Barometric Pressure			Precipitation Amount			
Rain	Sleet		Freezing Rain	Snow	Snow Depth	

Date			Sunrise		Sunset	
Sunny	Partly Cloudy		Cloudy	Wind Speed		
Temp Hi	Lo		Humidity		Dewpoint	
Barometric Pressure			Precipitation Amount			
Rain	Sleet		Freezing Rain	Snow	Snow Depth	

Weather Journal

Date		Sunrise		Sunset	
Sunny	Partly Cloudy	Cloudy	Wind Speed		
Temp Hi Lo		Humidity		Dewpoint	
Barometric Pressure		Precipitation Amount			
Rain	Sleet	Freezing Rain	Snow	Snow Depth	

Date		Sunrise		Sunset	
Sunny	Partly Cloudy	Cloudy	Wind Speed		
Temp Hi Lo		Humidity		Dewpoint	
Barometric Pressure		Precipitation Amount			
Rain	Sleet	Freezing Rain	Snow	Snow Depth	

Date		Sunrise		Sunset	
Sunny	Partly Cloudy	Cloudy	Wind Speed		
Temp Hi Lo		Humidity		Dewpoint	
Barometric Pressure		Precipitation Amount			
Rain	Sleet	Freezing Rain	Snow	Snow Depth	

Weather Journal

Date		Sunrise		Sunset	
Sunny	Partly Cloudy	Cloudy	Wind Speed		
Temp Hi	Lo	Humidity		Dewpoint	
Barometric Pressure		Precipitation Amount			
Rain	Sleet	Freezing Rain	Snow	Snow Depth	

Date		Sunrise		Sunset	
Sunny	Partly Cloudy	Cloudy	Wind Speed		
Temp Hi	Lo	Humidity		Dewpoint	
Barometric Pressure		Precipitation Amount			
Rain	Sleet	Freezing Rain	Snow	Snow Depth	

Date		Sunrise		Sunset	
Sunny	Partly Cloudy	Cloudy	Wind Speed		
Temp Hi	Lo	Humidity		Dewpoint	
Barometric Pressure		Precipitation Amount			
Rain	Sleet	Freezing Rain	Snow	Snow Depth	

Weather Journal

Date		Sunrise		Sunset
Sunny	Partly Cloudy	Cloudy	Wind Speed	
Temp Hi Lo		Humidity		Dewpoint
Barometric Pressure		Precipitation Amount		
Rain	Sleet	Freezing Rain	Snow	Snow Depth

Date		Sunrise		Sunset
Sunny	Partly Cloudy	Cloudy	Wind Speed	
Temp Hi Lo		Humidity		Dewpoint
Barometric Pressure		Precipitation Amount		
Rain	Sleet	Freezing Rain	Snow	Snow Depth

Date		Sunrise		Sunset
Sunny	Partly Cloudy	Cloudy	Wind Speed	
Temp Hi Lo		Humidity		Dewpoint
Barometric Pressure		Precipitation Amount		
Rain	Sleet	Freezing Rain	Snow	Snow Depth

Weather Journal

Date		Sunrise		Sunset	
Sunny	Partly Cloudy	Cloudy		Wind Speed	
Temp Hi	Lo	Humidity		Dewpoint	
Barometric Pressure		Precipitation Amount			
Rain	Sleet	Freezing Rain	Snow	Snow Depth	

Date		Sunrise		Sunset	
Sunny	Partly Cloudy	Cloudy		Wind Speed	
Temp Hi	Lo	Humidity		Dewpoint	
Barometric Pressure		Precipitation Amount			
Rain	Sleet	Freezing Rain	Snow	Snow Depth	

Date		Sunrise		Sunset	
Sunny	Partly Cloudy	Cloudy		Wind Speed	
Temp Hi	Lo	Humidity		Dewpoint	
Barometric Pressure		Precipitation Amount			
Rain	Sleet	Freezing Rain	Snow	Snow Depth	

Weather Journal

Date		Sunrise		Sunset	
Sunny	Partly Cloudy	Cloudy	Wind Speed		
Temp Hi Lo		Humidity		Dewpoint	
Barometric Pressure		Precipitation Amount			
Rain	Sleet	Freezing Rain	Snow	Snow Depth	

Date		Sunrise		Sunset	
Sunny	Partly Cloudy	Cloudy	Wind Speed		
Temp Hi Lo		Humidity		Dewpoint	
Barometric Pressure		Precipitation Amount			
Rain	Sleet	Freezing Rain	Snow	Snow Depth	

Date		Sunrise		Sunset	
Sunny	Partly Cloudy	Cloudy	Wind Speed		
Temp Hi Lo		Humidity		Dewpoint	
Barometric Pressure		Precipitation Amount			
Rain	Sleet	Freezing Rain	Snow	Snow Depth	

Weather Journal

Date		Sunrise		Sunset	
Sunny	Partly Cloudy	Cloudy	Wind Speed		
Temp Hi	Lo	Humidity		Dewpoint	
Barometric Pressure		Precipitation Amount			
Rain	Sleet	Freezing Rain	Snow	Snow Depth	

Date		Sunrise		Sunset	
Sunny	Partly Cloudy	Cloudy	Wind Speed		
Temp Hi	Lo	Humidity		Dewpoint	
Barometric Pressure		Precipitation Amount			
Rain	Sleet	Freezing Rain	Snow	Snow Depth	

Date		Sunrise		Sunset	
Sunny	Partly Cloudy	Cloudy	Wind Speed		
Temp Hi	Lo	Humidity		Dewpoint	
Barometric Pressure		Precipitation Amount			
Rain	Sleet	Freezing Rain	Snow	Snow Depth	

Weather Journal

Date		Sunrise		Sunset	
Sunny	Partly Cloudy	Cloudy	Wind Speed		
Temp Hi Lo		Humidity		Dewpoint	
Barometric Pressure		Precipitation Amount			
Rain	Sleet	Freezing Rain	Snow	Snow Depth	

Date		Sunrise		Sunset	
Sunny	Partly Cloudy	Cloudy	Wind Speed		
Temp Hi Lo		Humidity		Dewpoint	
Barometric Pressure		Precipitation Amount			
Rain	Sleet	Freezing Rain	Snow	Snow Depth	

Date		Sunrise		Sunset	
Sunny	Partly Cloudy	Cloudy	Wind Speed		
Temp Hi Lo		Humidity		Dewpoint	
Barometric Pressure		Precipitation Amount			
Rain	Sleet	Freezing Rain	Snow	Snow Depth	

Weather Journal

Date		Sunrise		Sunset	
Sunny	Partly Cloudy	Cloudy	Wind Speed		
Temp Hi Lo		Humidity		Dewpoint	
Barometric Pressure		Precipitation Amount			
Rain	Sleet	Freezing Rain	Snow	Snow Depth	

Date		Sunrise		Sunset	
Sunny	Partly Cloudy	Cloudy	Wind Speed		
Temp Hi Lo		Humidity		Dewpoint	
Barometric Pressure		Precipitation Amount			
Rain	Sleet	Freezing Rain	Snow	Snow Depth	

Date		Sunrise		Sunset	
Sunny	Partly Cloudy	Cloudy	Wind Speed		
Temp Hi Lo		Humidity		Dewpoint	
Barometric Pressure		Precipitation Amount			
Rain	Sleet	Freezing Rain	Snow	Snow Depth	

Weather Journal

Date		Sunrise		Sunset	
Sunny	Partly Cloudy	Cloudy	Wind Speed		
Temp Hi Lo		Humidity		Dewpoint	
Barometric Pressure		Precipitation Amount			
Rain	Sleet	Freezing Rain	Snow	Snow Depth	

Date		Sunrise		Sunset	
Sunny	Partly Cloudy	Cloudy	Wind Speed		
Temp Hi Lo		Humidity		Dewpoint	
Barometric Pressure		Precipitation Amount			
Rain	Sleet	Freezing Rain	Snow	Snow Depth	

Date		Sunrise		Sunset	
Sunny	Partly Cloudy	Cloudy	Wind Speed		
Temp Hi Lo		Humidity		Dewpoint	
Barometric Pressure		Precipitation Amount			
Rain	Sleet	Freezing Rain	Snow	Snow Depth	

Weather Journal

Date		Sunrise		Sunset	
Sunny	Partly Cloudy	Cloudy	Wind Speed		
Temp Hi Lo		Humidity		Dewpoint	
Barometric Pressure		Precipitation Amount			
Rain	Sleet	Freezing Rain	Snow	Snow Depth	

Date		Sunrise		Sunset	
Sunny	Partly Cloudy	Cloudy	Wind Speed		
Temp Hi Lo		Humidity		Dewpoint	
Barometric Pressure		Precipitation Amount			
Rain	Sleet	Freezing Rain	Snow	Snow Depth	

Date		Sunrise		Sunset	
Sunny	Partly Cloudy	Cloudy	Wind Speed		
Temp Hi Lo		Humidity		Dewpoint	
Barometric Pressure		Precipitation Amount			
Rain	Sleet	Freezing Rain	Snow	Snow Depth	

Weather Journal

Date		Sunrise		Sunset	
Sunny	Partly Cloudy	Cloudy	Wind Speed		
Temp Hi	Lo	Humidity		Dewpoint	
Barometric Pressure		Precipitation Amount			
Rain	Sleet	Freezing Rain	Snow	Snow Depth	

Date		Sunrise		Sunset	
Sunny	Partly Cloudy	Cloudy	Wind Speed		
Temp Hi	Lo	Humidity		Dewpoint	
Barometric Pressure		Precipitation Amount			
Rain	Sleet	Freezing Rain	Snow	Snow Depth	

Date		Sunrise		Sunset	
Sunny	Partly Cloudy	Cloudy	Wind Speed		
Temp Hi	Lo	Humidity		Dewpoint	
Barometric Pressure		Precipitation Amount			
Rain	Sleet	Freezing Rain	Snow	Snow Depth	

Weather Journal

Date			Sunrise		Sunset	
Sunny	Partly Cloudy		Cloudy	Wind Speed		
Temp Hi	Lo		Humidity		Dewpoint	
Barometric Pressure			Precipitation Amount			
Rain	Sleet		Freezing Rain	Snow	Snow Depth	

Date			Sunrise		Sunset	
Sunny	Partly Cloudy		Cloudy	Wind Speed		
Temp Hi	Lo		Humidity		Dewpoint	
Barometric Pressure			Precipitation Amount			
Rain	Sleet		Freezing Rain	Snow	Snow Depth	

Date			Sunrise		Sunset	
Sunny	Partly Cloudy		Cloudy	Wind Speed		
Temp Hi	Lo		Humidity		Dewpoint	
Barometric Pressure			Precipitation Amount			
Rain	Sleet		Freezing Rain	Snow	Snow Depth	

Weather Journal

Date		Sunrise		Sunset	
Sunny	Partly Cloudy	Cloudy	Wind Speed		
Temp Hi	Lo	Humidity		Dewpoint	
Barometric Pressure		Precipitation Amount			
Rain	Sleet	Freezing Rain	Snow	Snow Depth	

Date		Sunrise		Sunset	
Sunny	Partly Cloudy	Cloudy	Wind Speed		
Temp Hi	Lo	Humidity		Dewpoint	
Barometric Pressure		Precipitation Amount			
Rain	Sleet	Freezing Rain	Snow	Snow Depth	

Date		Sunrise		Sunset	
Sunny	Partly Cloudy	Cloudy	Wind Speed		
Temp Hi	Lo	Humidity		Dewpoint	
Barometric Pressure		Precipitation Amount			
Rain	Sleet	Freezing Rain	Snow	Snow Depth	

Weather Journal

Date		Sunrise		Sunset	
Sunny	Partly Cloudy	Cloudy	Wind Speed		
Temp Hi	Lo	Humidity		Dewpoint	
Barometric Pressure		Precipitation Amount			
Rain	Sleet	Freezing Rain	Snow	Snow Depth	

Date		Sunrise		Sunset	
Sunny	Partly Cloudy	Cloudy	Wind Speed		
Temp Hi	Lo	Humidity		Dewpoint	
Barometric Pressure		Precipitation Amount			
Rain	Sleet	Freezing Rain	Snow	Snow Depth	

Date		Sunrise		Sunset	
Sunny	Partly Cloudy	Cloudy	Wind Speed		
Temp Hi	Lo	Humidity		Dewpoint	
Barometric Pressure		Precipitation Amount			
Rain	Sleet	Freezing Rain	Snow	Snow Depth	

Weather Journal

Date		Sunrise		Sunset	
Sunny	Partly Cloudy	Cloudy	Wind Speed		
Temp Hi Lo		Humidity		Dewpoint	
Barometric Pressure		Precipitation Amount			
Rain	Sleet	Freezing Rain	Snow	Snow Depth	

Date		Sunrise		Sunset	
Sunny	Partly Cloudy	Cloudy	Wind Speed		
Temp Hi Lo		Humidity		Dewpoint	
Barometric Pressure		Precipitation Amount			
Rain	Sleet	Freezing Rain	Snow	Snow Depth	

Date		Sunrise		Sunset	
Sunny	Partly Cloudy	Cloudy	Wind Speed		
Temp Hi Lo		Humidity		Dewpoint	
Barometric Pressure		Precipitation Amount			
Rain	Sleet	Freezing Rain	Snow	Snow Depth	

Weather Journal

Date		Sunrise		Sunset	
Sunny	Partly Cloudy	Cloudy	Wind Speed		
Temp Hi	Lo	Humidity		Dewpoint	
Barometric Pressure		Precipitation Amount			
Rain	Sleet	Freezing Rain	Snow	Snow Depth	

Date		Sunrise		Sunset	
Sunny	Partly Cloudy	Cloudy	Wind Speed		
Temp Hi	Lo	Humidity		Dewpoint	
Barometric Pressure		Precipitation Amount			
Rain	Sleet	Freezing Rain	Snow	Snow Depth	

Date		Sunrise		Sunset	
Sunny	Partly Cloudy	Cloudy	Wind Speed		
Temp Hi	Lo	Humidity		Dewpoint	
Barometric Pressure		Precipitation Amount			
Rain	Sleet	Freezing Rain	Snow	Snow Depth	

Weather Journal

Date		Sunrise		Sunset	
Sunny	Partly Cloudy	Cloudy	Wind Speed		
Temp Hi	Lo	Humidity		Dewpoint	
Barometric Pressure		Precipitation Amount			
Rain	Sleet	Freezing Rain	Snow	Snow Depth	

Date		Sunrise		Sunset	
Sunny	Partly Cloudy	Cloudy	Wind Speed		
Temp Hi	Lo	Humidity		Dewpoint	
Barometric Pressure		Precipitation Amount			
Rain	Sleet	Freezing Rain	Snow	Snow Depth	

Date		Sunrise		Sunset	
Sunny	Partly Cloudy	Cloudy	Wind Speed		
Temp Hi	Lo	Humidity		Dewpoint	
Barometric Pressure		Precipitation Amount			
Rain	Sleet	Freezing Rain	Snow	Snow Depth	

Weather Journal

Date		Sunrise		Sunset	
Sunny	Partly Cloudy	Cloudy	Wind Speed		
Temp Hi Lo		Humidity		Dewpoint	
Barometric Pressure		Precipitation Amount			
Rain	Sleet	Freezing Rain	Snow	Snow Depth	

Date		Sunrise		Sunset	
Sunny	Partly Cloudy	Cloudy	Wind Speed		
Temp Hi Lo		Humidity		Dewpoint	
Barometric Pressure		Precipitation Amount			
Rain	Sleet	Freezing Rain	Snow	Snow Depth	

Date		Sunrise		Sunset	
Sunny	Partly Cloudy	Cloudy	Wind Speed		
Temp Hi Lo		Humidity		Dewpoint	
Barometric Pressure		Precipitation Amount			
Rain	Sleet	Freezing Rain	Snow	Snow Depth	

Weather Journal

Date		Sunrise		Sunset	
Sunny	Partly Cloudy	Cloudy	Wind Speed		
Temp Hi	Lo	Humidity		Dewpoint	
Barometric Pressure		Precipitation Amount			
Rain	Sleet	Freezing Rain	Snow	Snow Depth	

Date		Sunrise		Sunset	
Sunny	Partly Cloudy	Cloudy	Wind Speed		
Temp Hi	Lo	Humidity		Dewpoint	
Barometric Pressure		Precipitation Amount			
Rain	Sleet	Freezing Rain	Snow	Snow Depth	

Date		Sunrise		Sunset	
Sunny	Partly Cloudy	Cloudy	Wind Speed		
Temp Hi	Lo	Humidity		Dewpoint	
Barometric Pressure		Precipitation Amount			
Rain	Sleet	Freezing Rain	Snow	Snow Depth	

Weather Journal

Date		Sunrise		Sunset	
Sunny	Partly Cloudy	Cloudy	Wind Speed		
Temp Hi Lo		Humidity		Dewpoint	
Barometric Pressure		Precipitation Amount			
Rain	Sleet	Freezing Rain	Snow	Snow Depth	

Date		Sunrise		Sunset	
Sunny	Partly Cloudy	Cloudy	Wind Speed		
Temp Hi Lo		Humidity		Dewpoint	
Barometric Pressure		Precipitation Amount			
Rain	Sleet	Freezing Rain	Snow	Snow Depth	

Date		Sunrise		Sunset	
Sunny	Partly Cloudy	Cloudy	Wind Speed		
Temp Hi Lo		Humidity		Dewpoint	
Barometric Pressure		Precipitation Amount			
Rain	Sleet	Freezing Rain	Snow	Snow Depth	

Weather Journal

Date		Sunrise		Sunset	
Sunny	Partly Cloudy	Cloudy	Wind Speed		
Temp Hi Lo		Humidity		Dewpoint	
Barometric Pressure		Precipitation Amount			
Rain	Sleet	Freezing Rain	Snow	Snow Depth	

Date		Sunrise		Sunset	
Sunny	Partly Cloudy	Cloudy	Wind Speed		
Temp Hi Lo		Humidity		Dewpoint	
Barometric Pressure		Precipitation Amount			
Rain	Sleet	Freezing Rain	Snow	Snow Depth	

Date		Sunrise		Sunset	
Sunny	Partly Cloudy	Cloudy	Wind Speed		
Temp Hi Lo		Humidity		Dewpoint	
Barometric Pressure		Precipitation Amount			
Rain	Sleet	Freezing Rain	Snow	Snow Depth	

Weather Journal

Date		Sunrise		Sunset	
Sunny	Partly Cloudy	Cloudy	Wind Speed		
Temp Hi	Lo	Humidity		Dewpoint	
Barometric Pressure		Precipitation Amount			
Rain	Sleet	Freezing Rain	Snow	Snow Depth	

Date		Sunrise		Sunset	
Sunny	Partly Cloudy	Cloudy	Wind Speed		
Temp Hi	Lo	Humidity		Dewpoint	
Barometric Pressure		Precipitation Amount			
Rain	Sleet	Freezing Rain	Snow	Snow Depth	

Date		Sunrise		Sunset	
Sunny	Partly Cloudy	Cloudy	Wind Speed		
Temp Hi	Lo	Humidity		Dewpoint	
Barometric Pressure		Precipitation Amount			
Rain	Sleet	Freezing Rain	Snow	Snow Depth	

Weather Journal

Date		Sunrise		Sunset	
Sunny	Partly Cloudy	Cloudy	Wind Speed		
Temp Hi Lo		Humidity		Dewpoint	
Barometric Pressure		Precipitation Amount			
Rain	Sleet	Freezing Rain	Snow	Snow Depth	

Date		Sunrise		Sunset	
Sunny	Partly Cloudy	Cloudy	Wind Speed		
Temp Hi Lo		Humidity		Dewpoint	
Barometric Pressure		Precipitation Amount			
Rain	Sleet	Freezing Rain	Snow	Snow Depth	

Date		Sunrise		Sunset	
Sunny	Partly Cloudy	Cloudy	Wind Speed		
Temp Hi Lo		Humidity		Dewpoint	
Barometric Pressure		Precipitation Amount			
Rain	Sleet	Freezing Rain	Snow	Snow Depth	

Weather Journal

Date			Sunrise		Sunset	
Sunny	Partly Cloudy		Cloudy	Wind Speed		
Temp Hi	Lo		Humidity		Dewpoint	
Barometric Pressure			Precipitation Amount			
Rain	Sleet		Freezing Rain	Snow	Snow Depth	

Date			Sunrise		Sunset	
Sunny	Partly Cloudy		Cloudy	Wind Speed		
Temp Hi	Lo		Humidity		Dewpoint	
Barometric Pressure			Precipitation Amount			
Rain	Sleet		Freezing Rain	Snow	Snow Depth	

Date			Sunrise		Sunset	
Sunny	Partly Cloudy		Cloudy	Wind Speed		
Temp Hi	Lo		Humidity		Dewpoint	
Barometric Pressure			Precipitation Amount			
Rain	Sleet		Freezing Rain	Snow	Snow Depth	

Weather Journal

Date		Sunrise		Sunset	
Sunny	Partly Cloudy	Cloudy	Wind Speed		
Temp Hi	Lo	Humidity		Dewpoint	
Barometric Pressure		Precipitation Amount			
Rain	Sleet	Freezing Rain	Snow	Snow Depth	

Date		Sunrise		Sunset	
Sunny	Partly Cloudy	Cloudy	Wind Speed		
Temp Hi	Lo	Humidity		Dewpoint	
Barometric Pressure		Precipitation Amount			
Rain	Sleet	Freezing Rain	Snow	Snow Depth	

Date		Sunrise		Sunset	
Sunny	Partly Cloudy	Cloudy	Wind Speed		
Temp Hi	Lo	Humidity		Dewpoint	
Barometric Pressure		Precipitation Amount			
Rain	Sleet	Freezing Rain	Snow	Snow Depth	

Weather Journal

Date		Sunrise		Sunset	
Sunny	Partly Cloudy	Cloudy	Wind Speed		
Temp Hi	Lo	Humidity		Dewpoint	
Barometric Pressure		Precipitation Amount			
Rain	Sleet	Freezing Rain	Snow	Snow Depth	

Date		Sunrise		Sunset	
Sunny	Partly Cloudy	Cloudy	Wind Speed		
Temp Hi	Lo	Humidity		Dewpoint	
Barometric Pressure		Precipitation Amount			
Rain	Sleet	Freezing Rain	Snow	Snow Depth	

Date		Sunrise		Sunset	
Sunny	Partly Cloudy	Cloudy	Wind Speed		
Temp Hi	Lo	Humidity		Dewpoint	
Barometric Pressure		Precipitation Amount			
Rain	Sleet	Freezing Rain	Snow	Snow Depth	

Weather Journal

Date		Sunrise		Sunset	
Sunny	Partly Cloudy	Cloudy	Wind Speed		
Temp Hi Lo		Humidity		Dewpoint	
Barometric Pressure		Precipitation Amount			
Rain	Sleet	Freezing Rain	Snow	Snow Depth	

Date		Sunrise		Sunset	
Sunny	Partly Cloudy	Cloudy	Wind Speed		
Temp Hi Lo		Humidity		Dewpoint	
Barometric Pressure		Precipitation Amount			
Rain	Sleet	Freezing Rain	Snow	Snow Depth	

Date		Sunrise		Sunset	
Sunny	Partly Cloudy	Cloudy	Wind Speed		
Temp Hi Lo		Humidity		Dewpoint	
Barometric Pressure		Precipitation Amount			
Rain	Sleet	Freezing Rain	Snow	Snow Depth	

Weather Journal

Date		Sunrise		Sunset	
Sunny	Partly Cloudy	Cloudy	Wind Speed		
Temp Hi Lo		Humidity		Dewpoint	
Barometric Pressure		Precipitation Amount			
Rain	Sleet	Freezing Rain	Snow	Snow Depth	

Date		Sunrise		Sunset	
Sunny	Partly Cloudy	Cloudy	Wind Speed		
Temp Hi Lo		Humidity		Dewpoint	
Barometric Pressure		Precipitation Amount			
Rain	Sleet	Freezing Rain	Snow	Snow Depth	

Date		Sunrise		Sunset	
Sunny	Partly Cloudy	Cloudy	Wind Speed		
Temp Hi Lo		Humidity		Dewpoint	
Barometric Pressure		Precipitation Amount			
Rain	Sleet	Freezing Rain	Snow	Snow Depth	

Weather Journal

Date		Sunrise		Sunset	
Sunny	Partly Cloudy	Cloudy	Wind Speed		
Temp Hi Lo		Humidity		Dewpoint	
Barometric Pressure		Precipitation Amount			
Rain	Sleet	Freezing Rain	Snow	Snow Depth	

Date		Sunrise		Sunset	
Sunny	Partly Cloudy	Cloudy	Wind Speed		
Temp Hi Lo		Humidity		Dewpoint	
Barometric Pressure		Precipitation Amount			
Rain	Sleet	Freezing Rain	Snow	Snow Depth	

Date		Sunrise		Sunset	
Sunny	Partly Cloudy	Cloudy	Wind Speed		
Temp Hi Lo		Humidity		Dewpoint	
Barometric Pressure		Precipitation Amount			
Rain	Sleet	Freezing Rain	Snow	Snow Depth	

Weather Journal

Date		Sunrise		Sunset	
Sunny	Partly Cloudy	Cloudy	Wind Speed		
Temp Hi	Lo	Humidity		Dewpoint	
Barometric Pressure		Precipitation Amount			
Rain	Sleet	Freezing Rain	Snow	Snow Depth	

Date		Sunrise		Sunset	
Sunny	Partly Cloudy	Cloudy	Wind Speed		
Temp Hi	Lo	Humidity		Dewpoint	
Barometric Pressure		Precipitation Amount			
Rain	Sleet	Freezing Rain	Snow	Snow Depth	

Date		Sunrise		Sunset	
Sunny	Partly Cloudy	Cloudy	Wind Speed		
Temp Hi	Lo	Humidity		Dewpoint	
Barometric Pressure		Precipitation Amount			
Rain	Sleet	Freezing Rain	Snow	Snow Depth	

Weather Journal

Date			Sunrise		Sunset	
Sunny	Partly Cloudy		Cloudy	Wind Speed		
Temp Hi	Lo		Humidity		Dewpoint	
Barometric Pressure			Precipitation Amount			
Rain	Sleet		Freezing Rain	Snow	Snow Depth	

Date			Sunrise		Sunset	
Sunny	Partly Cloudy		Cloudy	Wind Speed		
Temp Hi	Lo		Humidity		Dewpoint	
Barometric Pressure			Precipitation Amount			
Rain	Sleet		Freezing Rain	Snow	Snow Depth	

Date			Sunrise		Sunset	
Sunny	Partly Cloudy		Cloudy	Wind Speed		
Temp Hi	Lo		Humidity		Dewpoint	
Barometric Pressure			Precipitation Amount			
Rain	Sleet		Freezing Rain	Snow	Snow Depth	

Weather Journal

Date			Sunrise		Sunset	
Sunny	Partly Cloudy		Cloudy	Wind Speed		
Temp Hi	Lo		Humidity		Dewpoint	
Barometric Pressure			Precipitation Amount			
Rain	Sleet		Freezing Rain	Snow	Snow Depth	

Date			Sunrise		Sunset	
Sunny	Partly Cloudy		Cloudy	Wind Speed		
Temp Hi	Lo		Humidity		Dewpoint	
Barometric Pressure			Precipitation Amount			
Rain	Sleet		Freezing Rain	Snow	Snow Depth	

Date			Sunrise		Sunset	
Sunny	Partly Cloudy		Cloudy	Wind Speed		
Temp Hi	Lo		Humidity		Dewpoint	
Barometric Pressure			Precipitation Amount			
Rain	Sleet		Freezing Rain	Snow	Snow Depth	

Weather Journal

Date		Sunrise		Sunset	
Sunny	Partly Cloudy	Cloudy	Wind Speed		
Temp Hi Lo		Humidity		Dewpoint	
Barometric Pressure		Precipitation Amount			
Rain	Sleet	Freezing Rain	Snow	Snow Depth	

Date		Sunrise		Sunset	
Sunny	Partly Cloudy	Cloudy	Wind Speed		
Temp Hi Lo		Humidity		Dewpoint	
Barometric Pressure		Precipitation Amount			
Rain	Sleet	Freezing Rain	Snow	Snow Depth	

Date		Sunrise		Sunset	
Sunny	Partly Cloudy	Cloudy	Wind Speed		
Temp Hi Lo		Humidity		Dewpoint	
Barometric Pressure		Precipitation Amount			
Rain	Sleet	Freezing Rain	Snow	Snow Depth	

Weather Journal

Date		Sunrise		Sunset	
Sunny	Partly Cloudy	Cloudy	Wind Speed		
Temp Hi Lo		Humidity		Dewpoint	
Barometric Pressure		Precipitation Amount			
Rain	Sleet	Freezing Rain	Snow	Snow Depth	

Date		Sunrise		Sunset	
Sunny	Partly Cloudy	Cloudy	Wind Speed		
Temp Hi Lo		Humidity		Dewpoint	
Barometric Pressure		Precipitation Amount			
Rain	Sleet	Freezing Rain	Snow	Snow Depth	

Date		Sunrise		Sunset	
Sunny	Partly Cloudy	Cloudy	Wind Speed		
Temp Hi Lo		Humidity		Dewpoint	
Barometric Pressure		Precipitation Amount			
Rain	Sleet	Freezing Rain	Snow	Snow Depth	

Weather Journal

Date		Sunrise		Sunset	
Sunny	Partly Cloudy	Cloudy	Wind Speed		
Temp Hi	Lo	Humidity		Dewpoint	
Barometric Pressure		Precipitation Amount			
Rain	Sleet	Freezing Rain	Snow	Snow Depth	

Date		Sunrise		Sunset	
Sunny	Partly Cloudy	Cloudy	Wind Speed		
Temp Hi	Lo	Humidity		Dewpoint	
Barometric Pressure		Precipitation Amount			
Rain	Sleet	Freezing Rain	Snow	Snow Depth	

Date		Sunrise		Sunset	
Sunny	Partly Cloudy	Cloudy	Wind Speed		
Temp Hi	Lo	Humidity		Dewpoint	
Barometric Pressure		Precipitation Amount			
Rain	Sleet	Freezing Rain	Snow	Snow Depth	

Weather Journal

Date		Sunrise		Sunset	
Sunny	Partly Cloudy	Cloudy	Wind Speed		
Temp Hi	Lo	Humidity		Dewpoint	
Barometric Pressure		Precipitation Amount			
Rain	Sleet	Freezing Rain	Snow	Snow Depth	

Date		Sunrise		Sunset	
Sunny	Partly Cloudy	Cloudy	Wind Speed		
Temp Hi	Lo	Humidity		Dewpoint	
Barometric Pressure		Precipitation Amount			
Rain	Sleet	Freezing Rain	Snow	Snow Depth	

Date		Sunrise		Sunset	
Sunny	Partly Cloudy	Cloudy	Wind Speed		
Temp Hi	Lo	Humidity		Dewpoint	
Barometric Pressure		Precipitation Amount			
Rain	Sleet	Freezing Rain	Snow	Snow Depth	

Weather Journal

Date		Sunrise		Sunset	
Sunny	Partly Cloudy	Cloudy	Wind Speed		
Temp Hi Lo		Humidity		Dewpoint	
Barometric Pressure		Precipitation Amount			
Rain	Sleet	Freezing Rain	Snow	Snow Depth	

Date		Sunrise		Sunset	
Sunny	Partly Cloudy	Cloudy	Wind Speed		
Temp Hi Lo		Humidity		Dewpoint	
Barometric Pressure		Precipitation Amount			
Rain	Sleet	Freezing Rain	Snow	Snow Depth	

Date		Sunrise		Sunset	
Sunny	Partly Cloudy	Cloudy	Wind Speed		
Temp Hi Lo		Humidity		Dewpoint	
Barometric Pressure		Precipitation Amount			
Rain	Sleet	Freezing Rain	Snow	Snow Depth	

Weather Journal

Date		Sunrise		Sunset	
Sunny	Partly Cloudy	Cloudy	Wind Speed		
Temp Hi	Lo	Humidity		Dewpoint	
Barometric Pressure		Precipitation Amount			
Rain	Sleet	Freezing Rain	Snow	Snow Depth	

Date		Sunrise		Sunset	
Sunny	Partly Cloudy	Cloudy	Wind Speed		
Temp Hi	Lo	Humidity		Dewpoint	
Barometric Pressure		Precipitation Amount			
Rain	Sleet	Freezing Rain	Snow	Snow Depth	

Date		Sunrise		Sunset	
Sunny	Partly Cloudy	Cloudy	Wind Speed		
Temp Hi	Lo	Humidity		Dewpoint	
Barometric Pressure		Precipitation Amount			
Rain	Sleet	Freezing Rain	Snow	Snow Depth	

Weather Journal

Date		Sunrise		Sunset	
Sunny	Partly Cloudy	Cloudy	Wind Speed		
Temp Hi Lo		Humidity		Dewpoint	
Barometric Pressure		Precipitation Amount			
Rain	Sleet	Freezing Rain	Snow	Snow Depth	

Date		Sunrise		Sunset	
Sunny	Partly Cloudy	Cloudy	Wind Speed		
Temp Hi Lo		Humidity		Dewpoint	
Barometric Pressure		Precipitation Amount			
Rain	Sleet	Freezing Rain	Snow	Snow Depth	

Date		Sunrise		Sunset	
Sunny	Partly Cloudy	Cloudy	Wind Speed		
Temp Hi Lo		Humidity		Dewpoint	
Barometric Pressure		Precipitation Amount			
Rain	Sleet	Freezing Rain	Snow	Snow Depth	

Weather Journal

Date		Sunrise		Sunset	
Sunny	Partly Cloudy	Cloudy	Wind Speed		
Temp Hi	Lo	Humidity		Dewpoint	
Barometric Pressure		Precipitation Amount			
Rain	Sleet	Freezing Rain	Snow	Snow Depth	

Date		Sunrise		Sunset	
Sunny	Partly Cloudy	Cloudy	Wind Speed		
Temp Hi	Lo	Humidity		Dewpoint	
Barometric Pressure		Precipitation Amount			
Rain	Sleet	Freezing Rain	Snow	Snow Depth	

Date		Sunrise		Sunset	
Sunny	Partly Cloudy	Cloudy	Wind Speed		
Temp Hi	Lo	Humidity		Dewpoint	
Barometric Pressure		Precipitation Amount			
Rain	Sleet	Freezing Rain	Snow	Snow Depth	

Weather Journal

Date			Sunrise		Sunset	
Sunny	Partly Cloudy		Cloudy	Wind Speed		
Temp Hi	Lo		Humidity		Dewpoint	
Barometric Pressure			Precipitation Amount			
Rain	Sleet		Freezing Rain	Snow	Snow Depth	

Date			Sunrise		Sunset	
Sunny	Partly Cloudy		Cloudy	Wind Speed		
Temp Hi	Lo		Humidity		Dewpoint	
Barometric Pressure			Precipitation Amount			
Rain	Sleet		Freezing Rain	Snow	Snow Depth	

Date			Sunrise		Sunset	
Sunny	Partly Cloudy		Cloudy	Wind Speed		
Temp Hi	Lo		Humidity		Dewpoint	
Barometric Pressure			Precipitation Amount			
Rain	Sleet		Freezing Rain	Snow	Snow Depth	

Weather Journal

Date		Sunrise		Sunset	
Sunny	Partly Cloudy	Cloudy	Wind Speed		
Temp Hi	Lo	Humidity		Dewpoint	
Barometric Pressure		Precipitation Amount			
Rain	Sleet	Freezing Rain	Snow	Snow Depth	

Date		Sunrise		Sunset	
Sunny	Partly Cloudy	Cloudy	Wind Speed		
Temp Hi	Lo	Humidity		Dewpoint	
Barometric Pressure		Precipitation Amount			
Rain	Sleet	Freezing Rain	Snow	Snow Depth	

Date		Sunrise		Sunset	
Sunny	Partly Cloudy	Cloudy	Wind Speed		
Temp Hi	Lo	Humidity		Dewpoint	
Barometric Pressure		Precipitation Amount			
Rain	Sleet	Freezing Rain	Snow	Snow Depth	

Weather Journal

Date		Sunrise		Sunset
Sunny	Partly Cloudy	Cloudy	Wind Speed	
Temp Hi	Lo	Humidity		Dewpoint
Barometric Pressure		Precipitation Amount		
Rain	Sleet	Freezing Rain	Snow	Snow Depth

Date		Sunrise		Sunset
Sunny	Partly Cloudy	Cloudy	Wind Speed	
Temp Hi	Lo	Humidity		Dewpoint
Barometric Pressure		Precipitation Amount		
Rain	Sleet	Freezing Rain	Snow	Snow Depth

Date		Sunrise		Sunset
Sunny	Partly Cloudy	Cloudy	Wind Speed	
Temp Hi	Lo	Humidity		Dewpoint
Barometric Pressure		Precipitation Amount		
Rain	Sleet	Freezing Rain	Snow	Snow Depth

Weather Journal

Date		Sunrise		Sunset	
Sunny	Partly Cloudy	Cloudy	Wind Speed		
Temp Hi Lo		Humidity		Dewpoint	
Barometric Pressure		Precipitation Amount			
Rain	Sleet	Freezing Rain	Snow	Snow Depth	

Date		Sunrise		Sunset	
Sunny	Partly Cloudy	Cloudy	Wind Speed		
Temp Hi Lo		Humidity		Dewpoint	
Barometric Pressure		Precipitation Amount			
Rain	Sleet	Freezing Rain	Snow	Snow Depth	

Date		Sunrise		Sunset	
Sunny	Partly Cloudy	Cloudy	Wind Speed		
Temp Hi Lo		Humidity		Dewpoint	
Barometric Pressure		Precipitation Amount			
Rain	Sleet	Freezing Rain	Snow	Snow Depth	

Weather Journal

Date			Sunrise		Sunset	
Sunny	Partly Cloudy		Cloudy	Wind Speed		
Temp Hi	Lo		Humidity		Dewpoint	
Barometric Pressure			Precipitation Amount			
Rain	Sleet		Freezing Rain	Snow	Snow Depth	

Date			Sunrise		Sunset	
Sunny	Partly Cloudy		Cloudy	Wind Speed		
Temp Hi	Lo		Humidity		Dewpoint	
Barometric Pressure			Precipitation Amount			
Rain	Sleet		Freezing Rain	Snow	Snow Depth	

Date			Sunrise		Sunset	
Sunny	Partly Cloudy		Cloudy	Wind Speed		
Temp Hi	Lo		Humidity		Dewpoint	
Barometric Pressure			Precipitation Amount			
Rain	Sleet		Freezing Rain	Snow	Snow Depth	

Weather Journal

Date		Sunrise		Sunset
Sunny	Partly Cloudy	Cloudy	Wind Speed	
Temp Hi	Lo	Humidity		Dewpoint
Barometric Pressure		Precipitation Amount		
Rain	Sleet	Freezing Rain	Snow	Snow Depth

Date		Sunrise		Sunset
Sunny	Partly Cloudy	Cloudy	Wind Speed	
Temp Hi	Lo	Humidity		Dewpoint
Barometric Pressure		Precipitation Amount		
Rain	Sleet	Freezing Rain	Snow	Snow Depth

Date		Sunrise		Sunset
Sunny	Partly Cloudy	Cloudy	Wind Speed	
Temp Hi	Lo	Humidity		Dewpoint
Barometric Pressure		Precipitation Amount		
Rain	Sleet	Freezing Rain	Snow	Snow Depth

Weather Journal

Date		Sunrise		Sunset	
Sunny	Partly Cloudy	Cloudy	Wind Speed		
Temp Hi Lo		Humidity		Dewpoint	
Barometric Pressure		Precipitation Amount			
Rain	Sleet	Freezing Rain	Snow	Snow Depth	

Date		Sunrise		Sunset	
Sunny	Partly Cloudy	Cloudy	Wind Speed		
Temp Hi Lo		Humidity		Dewpoint	
Barometric Pressure		Precipitation Amount			
Rain	Sleet	Freezing Rain	Snow	Snow Depth	

Date		Sunrise		Sunset	
Sunny	Partly Cloudy	Cloudy	Wind Speed		
Temp Hi Lo		Humidity		Dewpoint	
Barometric Pressure		Precipitation Amount			
Rain	Sleet	Freezing Rain	Snow	Snow Depth	

Weather Journal

Date		Sunrise		Sunset	
Sunny	Partly Cloudy	Cloudy	Wind Speed		
Temp Hi	Lo	Humidity		Dewpoint	
Barometric Pressure		Precipitation Amount			
Rain	Sleet	Freezing Rain	Snow	Snow Depth	

Date		Sunrise		Sunset	
Sunny	Partly Cloudy	Cloudy	Wind Speed		
Temp Hi	Lo	Humidity		Dewpoint	
Barometric Pressure		Precipitation Amount			
Rain	Sleet	Freezing Rain	Snow	Snow Depth	

Date		Sunrise		Sunset	
Sunny	Partly Cloudy	Cloudy	Wind Speed		
Temp Hi	Lo	Humidity		Dewpoint	
Barometric Pressure		Precipitation Amount			
Rain	Sleet	Freezing Rain	Snow	Snow Depth	

Weather Journal

Date		Sunrise		Sunset	
Sunny	Partly Cloudy	Cloudy	Wind Speed		
Temp Hi	Lo	Humidity		Dewpoint	
Barometric Pressure		Precipitation Amount			
Rain	Sleet	Freezing Rain	Snow	Snow Depth	

Date		Sunrise		Sunset	
Sunny	Partly Cloudy	Cloudy	Wind Speed		
Temp Hi	Lo	Humidity		Dewpoint	
Barometric Pressure		Precipitation Amount			
Rain	Sleet	Freezing Rain	Snow	Snow Depth	

Date		Sunrise		Sunset	
Sunny	Partly Cloudy	Cloudy	Wind Speed		
Temp Hi	Lo	Humidity		Dewpoint	
Barometric Pressure		Precipitation Amount			
Rain	Sleet	Freezing Rain	Snow	Snow Depth	

Weather Journal

Date		Sunrise		Sunset	
Sunny	Partly Cloudy	Cloudy	Wind Speed		
Temp Hi Lo		Humidity		Dewpoint	
Barometric Pressure		Precipitation Amount			
Rain	Sleet	Freezing Rain	Snow	Snow Depth	

Date		Sunrise		Sunset	
Sunny	Partly Cloudy	Cloudy	Wind Speed		
Temp Hi Lo		Humidity		Dewpoint	
Barometric Pressure		Precipitation Amount			
Rain	Sleet	Freezing Rain	Snow	Snow Depth	

Date		Sunrise		Sunset	
Sunny	Partly Cloudy	Cloudy	Wind Speed		
Temp Hi Lo		Humidity		Dewpoint	
Barometric Pressure		Precipitation Amount			
Rain	Sleet	Freezing Rain	Snow	Snow Depth	

Weather Journal

Date		Sunrise		Sunset	
Sunny	Partly Cloudy	Cloudy	Wind Speed		
Temp Hi Lo		Humidity		Dewpoint	
Barometric Pressure		Precipitation Amount			
Rain	Sleet	Freezing Rain	Snow	Snow Depth	

Date		Sunrise		Sunset	
Sunny	Partly Cloudy	Cloudy	Wind Speed		
Temp Hi Lo		Humidity		Dewpoint	
Barometric Pressure		Precipitation Amount			
Rain	Sleet	Freezing Rain	Snow	Snow Depth	

Date		Sunrise		Sunset	
Sunny	Partly Cloudy	Cloudy	Wind Speed		
Temp Hi Lo		Humidity		Dewpoint	
Barometric Pressure		Precipitation Amount			
Rain	Sleet	Freezing Rain	Snow	Snow Depth	

Weather Journal

Date		Sunrise		Sunset	
Sunny	Partly Cloudy	Cloudy	Wind Speed		
Temp Hi	Lo	Humidity		Dewpoint	
Barometric Pressure		Precipitation Amount			
Rain	Sleet	Freezing Rain	Snow	Snow Depth	

Date		Sunrise		Sunset	
Sunny	Partly Cloudy	Cloudy	Wind Speed		
Temp Hi	Lo	Humidity		Dewpoint	
Barometric Pressure		Precipitation Amount			
Rain	Sleet	Freezing Rain	Snow	Snow Depth	

Date		Sunrise		Sunset	
Sunny	Partly Cloudy	Cloudy	Wind Speed		
Temp Hi	Lo	Humidity		Dewpoint	
Barometric Pressure		Precipitation Amount			
Rain	Sleet	Freezing Rain	Snow	Snow Depth	

Weather Journal

Date		Sunrise		Sunset	
Sunny	Partly Cloudy	Cloudy	Wind Speed		
Temp Hi Lo		Humidity		Dewpoint	
Barometric Pressure		Precipitation Amount			
Rain	Sleet	Freezing Rain	Snow	Snow Depth	

Date		Sunrise		Sunset	
Sunny	Partly Cloudy	Cloudy	Wind Speed		
Temp Hi Lo		Humidity		Dewpoint	
Barometric Pressure		Precipitation Amount			
Rain	Sleet	Freezing Rain	Snow	Snow Depth	

Date		Sunrise		Sunset	
Sunny	Partly Cloudy	Cloudy	Wind Speed		
Temp Hi Lo		Humidity		Dewpoint	
Barometric Pressure		Precipitation Amount			
Rain	Sleet	Freezing Rain	Snow	Snow Depth	

Weather Journal

Date		Sunrise		Sunset	
Sunny	Partly Cloudy	Cloudy	Wind Speed		
Temp Hi Lo		Humidity		Dewpoint	
Barometric Pressure		Precipitation Amount			
Rain	Sleet	Freezing Rain	Snow	Snow Depth	

Date		Sunrise		Sunset	
Sunny	Partly Cloudy	Cloudy	Wind Speed		
Temp Hi Lo		Humidity		Dewpoint	
Barometric Pressure		Precipitation Amount			
Rain	Sleet	Freezing Rain	Snow	Snow Depth	

Date		Sunrise		Sunset	
Sunny	Partly Cloudy	Cloudy	Wind Speed		
Temp Hi Lo		Humidity		Dewpoint	
Barometric Pressure		Precipitation Amount			
Rain	Sleet	Freezing Rain	Snow	Snow Depth	

Weather Journal

Date		Sunrise		Sunset	
Sunny	Partly Cloudy	Cloudy	Wind Speed		
Temp Hi Lo		Humidity		Dewpoint	
Barometric Pressure		Precipitation Amount			
Rain	Sleet	Freezing Rain	Snow	Snow Depth	

Date		Sunrise		Sunset	
Sunny	Partly Cloudy	Cloudy	Wind Speed		
Temp Hi Lo		Humidity		Dewpoint	
Barometric Pressure		Precipitation Amount			
Rain	Sleet	Freezing Rain	Snow	Snow Depth	

Date		Sunrise		Sunset	
Sunny	Partly Cloudy	Cloudy	Wind Speed		
Temp Hi Lo		Humidity		Dewpoint	
Barometric Pressure		Precipitation Amount			
Rain	Sleet	Freezing Rain	Snow	Snow Depth	

Weather Journal

Date		Sunrise		Sunset	
Sunny	Partly Cloudy	Cloudy	Wind Speed		
Temp Hi	Lo	Humidity		Dewpoint	
Barometric Pressure		Precipitation Amount			
Rain	Sleet	Freezing Rain	Snow	Snow Depth	

Date		Sunrise		Sunset	
Sunny	Partly Cloudy	Cloudy	Wind Speed		
Temp Hi	Lo	Humidity		Dewpoint	
Barometric Pressure		Precipitation Amount			
Rain	Sleet	Freezing Rain	Snow	Snow Depth	

Date		Sunrise		Sunset	
Sunny	Partly Cloudy	Cloudy	Wind Speed		
Temp Hi	Lo	Humidity		Dewpoint	
Barometric Pressure		Precipitation Amount			
Rain	Sleet	Freezing Rain	Snow	Snow Depth	

Weather Journal

Date		Sunrise		Sunset	
Sunny	Partly Cloudy	Cloudy	Wind Speed		
Temp Hi Lo		Humidity		Dewpoint	
Barometric Pressure		Precipitation Amount			
Rain	Sleet	Freezing Rain	Snow	Snow Depth	

Date		Sunrise		Sunset	
Sunny	Partly Cloudy	Cloudy	Wind Speed		
Temp Hi Lo		Humidity		Dewpoint	
Barometric Pressure		Precipitation Amount			
Rain	Sleet	Freezing Rain	Snow	Snow Depth	

Date		Sunrise		Sunset	
Sunny	Partly Cloudy	Cloudy	Wind Speed		
Temp Hi Lo		Humidity		Dewpoint	
Barometric Pressure		Precipitation Amount			
Rain	Sleet	Freezing Rain	Snow	Snow Depth	

Weather Journal

Date		Sunrise		Sunset	
Sunny	Partly Cloudy	Cloudy	Wind Speed		
Temp Hi	Lo	Humidity		Dewpoint	
Barometric Pressure		Precipitation Amount			
Rain	Sleet	Freezing Rain	Snow	Snow Depth	

Date		Sunrise		Sunset	
Sunny	Partly Cloudy	Cloudy	Wind Speed		
Temp Hi	Lo	Humidity		Dewpoint	
Barometric Pressure		Precipitation Amount			
Rain	Sleet	Freezing Rain	Snow	Snow Depth	

Date		Sunrise		Sunset	
Sunny	Partly Cloudy	Cloudy	Wind Speed		
Temp Hi	Lo	Humidity		Dewpoint	
Barometric Pressure		Precipitation Amount			
Rain	Sleet	Freezing Rain	Snow	Snow Depth	

Weather Journal

Date		Sunrise		Sunset	
Sunny	Partly Cloudy	Cloudy	Wind Speed		
Temp Hi Lo		Humidity		Dewpoint	
Barometric Pressure		Precipitation Amount			
Rain	Sleet	Freezing Rain	Snow	Snow Depth	

Date		Sunrise		Sunset	
Sunny	Partly Cloudy	Cloudy	Wind Speed		
Temp Hi Lo		Humidity		Dewpoint	
Barometric Pressure		Precipitation Amount			
Rain	Sleet	Freezing Rain	Snow	Snow Depth	

Date		Sunrise		Sunset	
Sunny	Partly Cloudy	Cloudy	Wind Speed		
Temp Hi Lo		Humidity		Dewpoint	
Barometric Pressure		Precipitation Amount			
Rain	Sleet	Freezing Rain	Snow	Snow Depth	

Weather Journal

Date		Sunrise		Sunset	
Sunny	Partly Cloudy	Cloudy	Wind Speed		
Temp Hi	Lo	Humidity		Dewpoint	
Barometric Pressure		Precipitation Amount			
Rain	Sleet	Freezing Rain	Snow	Snow Depth	

Date		Sunrise		Sunset	
Sunny	Partly Cloudy	Cloudy	Wind Speed		
Temp Hi	Lo	Humidity		Dewpoint	
Barometric Pressure		Precipitation Amount			
Rain	Sleet	Freezing Rain	Snow	Snow Depth	

Date		Sunrise		Sunset	
Sunny	Partly Cloudy	Cloudy	Wind Speed		
Temp Hi	Lo	Humidity		Dewpoint	
Barometric Pressure		Precipitation Amount			
Rain	Sleet	Freezing Rain	Snow	Snow Depth	

Weather Journal

Date		Sunrise		Sunset	
Sunny	Partly Cloudy	Cloudy	Wind Speed		
Temp Hi Lo		Humidity		Dewpoint	
Barometric Pressure		Precipitation Amount			
Rain	Sleet	Freezing Rain	Snow	Snow Depth	

Date		Sunrise		Sunset	
Sunny	Partly Cloudy	Cloudy	Wind Speed		
Temp Hi Lo		Humidity		Dewpoint	
Barometric Pressure		Precipitation Amount			
Rain	Sleet	Freezing Rain	Snow	Snow Depth	

Date		Sunrise		Sunset	
Sunny	Partly Cloudy	Cloudy	Wind Speed		
Temp Hi Lo		Humidity		Dewpoint	
Barometric Pressure		Precipitation Amount			
Rain	Sleet	Freezing Rain	Snow	Snow Depth	

Weather Journal

Date		Sunrise		Sunset	
Sunny	Partly Cloudy	Cloudy	Wind Speed		
Temp Hi	Lo	Humidity		Dewpoint	
Barometric Pressure		Precipitation Amount			
Rain	Sleet	Freezing Rain	Snow	Snow Depth	

Date		Sunrise		Sunset	
Sunny	Partly Cloudy	Cloudy	Wind Speed		
Temp Hi	Lo	Humidity		Dewpoint	
Barometric Pressure		Precipitation Amount			
Rain	Sleet	Freezing Rain	Snow	Snow Depth	

Date		Sunrise		Sunset	
Sunny	Partly Cloudy	Cloudy	Wind Speed		
Temp Hi	Lo	Humidity		Dewpoint	
Barometric Pressure		Precipitation Amount			
Rain	Sleet	Freezing Rain	Snow	Snow Depth	

Weather Journal

Date		Sunrise		Sunset	
Sunny	Partly Cloudy	Cloudy	Wind Speed		
Temp Hi Lo		Humidity		Dewpoint	
Barometric Pressure		Precipitation Amount			
Rain	Sleet	Freezing Rain	Snow	Snow Depth	

Date		Sunrise		Sunset	
Sunny	Partly Cloudy	Cloudy	Wind Speed		
Temp Hi Lo		Humidity		Dewpoint	
Barometric Pressure		Precipitation Amount			
Rain	Sleet	Freezing Rain	Snow	Snow Depth	

Date		Sunrise		Sunset	
Sunny	Partly Cloudy	Cloudy	Wind Speed		
Temp Hi Lo		Humidity		Dewpoint	
Barometric Pressure		Precipitation Amount			
Rain	Sleet	Freezing Rain	Snow	Snow Depth	

Weather Journal

Date		Sunrise		Sunset	
Sunny	Partly Cloudy	Cloudy	Wind Speed		
Temp Hi Lo		Humidity		Dewpoint	
Barometric Pressure		Precipitation Amount			
Rain	Sleet	Freezing Rain	Snow	Snow Depth	

Date		Sunrise		Sunset	
Sunny	Partly Cloudy	Cloudy	Wind Speed		
Temp Hi Lo		Humidity		Dewpoint	
Barometric Pressure		Precipitation Amount			
Rain	Sleet	Freezing Rain	Snow	Snow Depth	

Date		Sunrise		Sunset	
Sunny	Partly Cloudy	Cloudy	Wind Speed		
Temp Hi Lo		Humidity		Dewpoint	
Barometric Pressure		Precipitation Amount			
Rain	Sleet	Freezing Rain	Snow	Snow Depth	

Weather Journal

Date		Sunrise		Sunset	
Sunny	Partly Cloudy	Cloudy	Wind Speed		
Temp Hi	Lo	Humidity		Dewpoint	
Barometric Pressure		Precipitation Amount			
Rain	Sleet	Freezing Rain	Snow	Snow Depth	

Date		Sunrise		Sunset	
Sunny	Partly Cloudy	Cloudy	Wind Speed		
Temp Hi	Lo	Humidity		Dewpoint	
Barometric Pressure		Precipitation Amount			
Rain	Sleet	Freezing Rain	Snow	Snow Depth	

Date		Sunrise		Sunset	
Sunny	Partly Cloudy	Cloudy	Wind Speed		
Temp Hi	Lo	Humidity		Dewpoint	
Barometric Pressure		Precipitation Amount			
Rain	Sleet	Freezing Rain	Snow	Snow Depth	

Weather Journal

Date			Sunrise		Sunset	
Sunny	Partly Cloudy		Cloudy	Wind Speed		
Temp Hi	Lo		Humidity		Dewpoint	
Barometric Pressure			Precipitation Amount			
Rain	Sleet		Freezing Rain	Snow	Snow Depth	

Date			Sunrise		Sunset	
Sunny	Partly Cloudy		Cloudy	Wind Speed		
Temp Hi	Lo		Humidity		Dewpoint	
Barometric Pressure			Precipitation Amount			
Rain	Sleet		Freezing Rain	Snow	Snow Depth	

Date			Sunrise		Sunset	
Sunny	Partly Cloudy		Cloudy	Wind Speed		
Temp Hi	Lo		Humidity		Dewpoint	
Barometric Pressure			Precipitation Amount			
Rain	Sleet		Freezing Rain	Snow	Snow Depth	

Weather Journal

Date		Sunrise		Sunset	
Sunny	Partly Cloudy	Cloudy	Wind Speed		
Temp Hi	Lo	Humidity		Dewpoint	
Barometric Pressure		Precipitation Amount			
Rain	Sleet	Freezing Rain	Snow	Snow Depth	

Date		Sunrise		Sunset	
Sunny	Partly Cloudy	Cloudy	Wind Speed		
Temp Hi	Lo	Humidity		Dewpoint	
Barometric Pressure		Precipitation Amount			
Rain	Sleet	Freezing Rain	Snow	Snow Depth	

Date		Sunrise		Sunset	
Sunny	Partly Cloudy	Cloudy	Wind Speed		
Temp Hi	Lo	Humidity		Dewpoint	
Barometric Pressure		Precipitation Amount			
Rain	Sleet	Freezing Rain	Snow	Snow Depth	

Weather Journal

Date		Sunrise		Sunset	
Sunny	Partly Cloudy	Cloudy	Wind Speed		
Temp Hi	Lo	Humidity		Dewpoint	
Barometric Pressure		Precipitation Amount			
Rain	Sleet	Freezing Rain	Snow	Snow Depth	

Date		Sunrise		Sunset	
Sunny	Partly Cloudy	Cloudy	Wind Speed		
Temp Hi	Lo	Humidity		Dewpoint	
Barometric Pressure		Precipitation Amount			
Rain	Sleet	Freezing Rain	Snow	Snow Depth	

Date		Sunrise		Sunset	
Sunny	Partly Cloudy	Cloudy	Wind Speed		
Temp Hi	Lo	Humidity		Dewpoint	
Barometric Pressure		Precipitation Amount			
Rain	Sleet	Freezing Rain	Snow	Snow Depth	

Weather Journal

Date		Sunrise		Sunset	
Sunny	Partly Cloudy	Cloudy	Wind Speed		
Temp Hi Lo		Humidity		Dewpoint	
Barometric Pressure		Precipitation Amount			
Rain	Sleet	Freezing Rain	Snow	Snow Depth	

Date		Sunrise		Sunset	
Sunny	Partly Cloudy	Cloudy	Wind Speed		
Temp Hi Lo		Humidity		Dewpoint	
Barometric Pressure		Precipitation Amount			
Rain	Sleet	Freezing Rain	Snow	Snow Depth	

Date		Sunrise		Sunset	
Sunny	Partly Cloudy	Cloudy	Wind Speed		
Temp Hi Lo		Humidity		Dewpoint	
Barometric Pressure		Precipitation Amount			
Rain	Sleet	Freezing Rain	Snow	Snow Depth	

Weather Journal

Date			Sunrise		Sunset	
Sunny	Partly Cloudy		Cloudy	Wind Speed		
Temp Hi	Lo		Humidity		Dewpoint	
Barometric Pressure			Precipitation Amount			
Rain	Sleet		Freezing Rain	Snow	Snow Depth	

Date			Sunrise		Sunset	
Sunny	Partly Cloudy		Cloudy	Wind Speed		
Temp Hi	Lo		Humidity		Dewpoint	
Barometric Pressure			Precipitation Amount			
Rain	Sleet		Freezing Rain	Snow	Snow Depth	

Date			Sunrise		Sunset	
Sunny	Partly Cloudy		Cloudy	Wind Speed		
Temp Hi	Lo		Humidity		Dewpoint	
Barometric Pressure			Precipitation Amount			
Rain	Sleet		Freezing Rain	Snow	Snow Depth	

Weather Journal

Date		Sunrise		Sunset	
Sunny	Partly Cloudy	Cloudy	Wind Speed		
Temp Hi Lo		Humidity		Dewpoint	
Barometric Pressure		Precipitation Amount			
Rain	Sleet	Freezing Rain	Snow	Snow Depth	

Date		Sunrise		Sunset	
Sunny	Partly Cloudy	Cloudy	Wind Speed		
Temp Hi Lo		Humidity		Dewpoint	
Barometric Pressure		Precipitation Amount			
Rain	Sleet	Freezing Rain	Snow	Snow Depth	

Date		Sunrise		Sunset	
Sunny	Partly Cloudy	Cloudy	Wind Speed		
Temp Hi Lo		Humidity		Dewpoint	
Barometric Pressure		Precipitation Amount			
Rain	Sleet	Freezing Rain	Snow	Snow Depth	

Weather Journal

Date		Sunrise		Sunset	
Sunny	Partly Cloudy	Cloudy	Wind Speed		
Temp Hi	Lo	Humidity		Dewpoint	
Barometric Pressure		Precipitation Amount			
Rain	Sleet	Freezing Rain	Snow	Snow Depth	

Date		Sunrise		Sunset	
Sunny	Partly Cloudy	Cloudy	Wind Speed		
Temp Hi	Lo	Humidity		Dewpoint	
Barometric Pressure		Precipitation Amount			
Rain	Sleet	Freezing Rain	Snow	Snow Depth	

Date		Sunrise		Sunset	
Sunny	Partly Cloudy	Cloudy	Wind Speed		
Temp Hi	Lo	Humidity		Dewpoint	
Barometric Pressure		Precipitation Amount			
Rain	Sleet	Freezing Rain	Snow	Snow Depth	

Weather Journal

Date		Sunrise		Sunset	
Sunny	Partly Cloudy	Cloudy	Wind Speed		
Temp Hi	Lo	Humidity		Dewpoint	
Barometric Pressure		Precipitation Amount			
Rain	Sleet	Freezing Rain	Snow	Snow Depth	

Date		Sunrise		Sunset	
Sunny	Partly Cloudy	Cloudy	Wind Speed		
Temp Hi	Lo	Humidity		Dewpoint	
Barometric Pressure		Precipitation Amount			
Rain	Sleet	Freezing Rain	Snow	Snow Depth	

Date		Sunrise		Sunset	
Sunny	Partly Cloudy	Cloudy	Wind Speed		
Temp Hi	Lo	Humidity		Dewpoint	
Barometric Pressure		Precipitation Amount			
Rain	Sleet	Freezing Rain	Snow	Snow Depth	

Weather Journal

Date		Sunrise		Sunset	
Sunny	Partly Cloudy	Cloudy	Wind Speed		
Temp Hi	Lo	Humidity		Dewpoint	
Barometric Pressure		Precipitation Amount			
Rain	Sleet	Freezing Rain	Snow	Snow Depth	

Date		Sunrise		Sunset	
Sunny	Partly Cloudy	Cloudy	Wind Speed		
Temp Hi	Lo	Humidity		Dewpoint	
Barometric Pressure		Precipitation Amount			
Rain	Sleet	Freezing Rain	Snow	Snow Depth	

Date		Sunrise		Sunset	
Sunny	Partly Cloudy	Cloudy	Wind Speed		
Temp Hi	Lo	Humidity		Dewpoint	
Barometric Pressure		Precipitation Amount			
Rain	Sleet	Freezing Rain	Snow	Snow Depth	

Weather Journal

Date		Sunrise		Sunset	
Sunny	Partly Cloudy	Cloudy	Wind Speed		
Temp Hi Lo		Humidity		Dewpoint	
Barometric Pressure		Precipitation Amount			
Rain	Sleet	Freezing Rain	Snow	Snow Depth	

Date		Sunrise		Sunset	
Sunny	Partly Cloudy	Cloudy	Wind Speed		
Temp Hi Lo		Humidity		Dewpoint	
Barometric Pressure		Precipitation Amount			
Rain	Sleet	Freezing Rain	Snow	Snow Depth	

Date		Sunrise		Sunset	
Sunny	Partly Cloudy	Cloudy	Wind Speed		
Temp Hi Lo		Humidity		Dewpoint	
Barometric Pressure		Precipitation Amount			
Rain	Sleet	Freezing Rain	Snow	Snow Depth	

Weather Journal

Date			Sunrise		Sunset	
Sunny	Partly Cloudy		Cloudy	Wind Speed		
Temp Hi	Lo		Humidity		Dewpoint	
Barometric Pressure			Precipitation Amount			
Rain	Sleet		Freezing Rain	Snow	Snow Depth	

Date			Sunrise		Sunset	
Sunny	Partly Cloudy		Cloudy	Wind Speed		
Temp Hi	Lo		Humidity		Dewpoint	
Barometric Pressure			Precipitation Amount			
Rain	Sleet		Freezing Rain	Snow	Snow Depth	

Date			Sunrise		Sunset	
Sunny	Partly Cloudy		Cloudy	Wind Speed		
Temp Hi	Lo		Humidity		Dewpoint	
Barometric Pressure			Precipitation Amount			
Rain	Sleet		Freezing Rain	Snow	Snow Depth	

Weather Journal

Date		Sunrise		Sunset	
Sunny	Partly Cloudy	Cloudy	Wind Speed		
Temp Hi	Lo	Humidity		Dewpoint	
Barometric Pressure		Precipitation Amount			
Rain	Sleet	Freezing Rain	Snow	Snow Depth	

Date		Sunrise		Sunset	
Sunny	Partly Cloudy	Cloudy	Wind Speed		
Temp Hi	Lo	Humidity		Dewpoint	
Barometric Pressure		Precipitation Amount			
Rain	Sleet	Freezing Rain	Snow	Snow Depth	

Date		Sunrise		Sunset	
Sunny	Partly Cloudy	Cloudy	Wind Speed		
Temp Hi	Lo	Humidity		Dewpoint	
Barometric Pressure		Precipitation Amount			
Rain	Sleet	Freezing Rain	Snow	Snow Depth	

Weather Journal

Date		Sunrise		Sunset	
Sunny	Partly Cloudy	Cloudy		Wind Speed	
Temp Hi Lo		Humidity		Dewpoint	
Barometric Pressure		Precipitation Amount			
Rain	Sleet	Freezing Rain		Snow	Snow Depth

Date		Sunrise		Sunset	
Sunny	Partly Cloudy	Cloudy		Wind Speed	
Temp Hi Lo		Humidity		Dewpoint	
Barometric Pressure		Precipitation Amount			
Rain	Sleet	Freezing Rain		Snow	Snow Depth

Date		Sunrise		Sunset	
Sunny	Partly Cloudy	Cloudy		Wind Speed	
Temp Hi Lo		Humidity		Dewpoint	
Barometric Pressure		Precipitation Amount			
Rain	Sleet	Freezing Rain		Snow	Snow Depth

Weather Journal

Date		Sunrise		Sunset	
Sunny	Partly Cloudy	Cloudy	Wind Speed		
Temp Hi	Lo	Humidity		Dewpoint	
Barometric Pressure		Precipitation Amount			
Rain	Sleet	Freezing Rain	Snow	Snow Depth	

Date		Sunrise		Sunset	
Sunny	Partly Cloudy	Cloudy	Wind Speed		
Temp Hi	Lo	Humidity		Dewpoint	
Barometric Pressure		Precipitation Amount			
Rain	Sleet	Freezing Rain	Snow	Snow Depth	

Date		Sunrise		Sunset	
Sunny	Partly Cloudy	Cloudy	Wind Speed		
Temp Hi	Lo	Humidity		Dewpoint	
Barometric Pressure		Precipitation Amount			
Rain	Sleet	Freezing Rain	Snow	Snow Depth	

Weather Journal

Date			Sunrise		Sunset	
Sunny	Partly Cloudy		Cloudy	Wind Speed		
Temp Hi		Lo	Humidity		Dewpoint	
Barometric Pressure			Precipitation Amount			
Rain		Sleet	Freezing Rain	Snow	Snow Depth	

Date			Sunrise		Sunset	
Sunny	Partly Cloudy		Cloudy	Wind Speed		
Temp Hi		Lo	Humidity		Dewpoint	
Barometric Pressure			Precipitation Amount			
Rain		Sleet	Freezing Rain	Snow	Snow Depth	

Date			Sunrise		Sunset	
Sunny	Partly Cloudy		Cloudy	Wind Speed		
Temp Hi		Lo	Humidity		Dewpoint	
Barometric Pressure			Precipitation Amount			
Rain		Sleet	Freezing Rain	Snow	Snow Depth	

Weather Journal

Date		Sunrise		Sunset	
Sunny	Partly Cloudy	Cloudy	Wind Speed		
Temp Hi	Lo	Humidity		Dewpoint	
Barometric Pressure		Precipitation Amount			
Rain	Sleet	Freezing Rain	Snow	Snow Depth	

Date		Sunrise		Sunset	
Sunny	Partly Cloudy	Cloudy	Wind Speed		
Temp Hi	Lo	Humidity		Dewpoint	
Barometric Pressure		Precipitation Amount			
Rain	Sleet	Freezing Rain	Snow	Snow Depth	

Date		Sunrise		Sunset	
Sunny	Partly Cloudy	Cloudy	Wind Speed		
Temp Hi	Lo	Humidity		Dewpoint	
Barometric Pressure		Precipitation Amount			
Rain	Sleet	Freezing Rain	Snow	Snow Depth	

Weather Journal

Date			Sunrise		Sunset	
Sunny	Partly Cloudy		Cloudy	Wind Speed		
Temp Hi	Lo		Humidity		Dewpoint	
Barometric Pressure			Precipitation Amount			
Rain	Sleet		Freezing Rain	Snow	Snow Depth	

Date			Sunrise		Sunset	
Sunny	Partly Cloudy		Cloudy	Wind Speed		
Temp Hi	Lo		Humidity		Dewpoint	
Barometric Pressure			Precipitation Amount			
Rain	Sleet		Freezing Rain	Snow	Snow Depth	

Date			Sunrise		Sunset	
Sunny	Partly Cloudy		Cloudy	Wind Speed		
Temp Hi	Lo		Humidity		Dewpoint	
Barometric Pressure			Precipitation Amount			
Rain	Sleet		Freezing Rain	Snow	Snow Depth	

Weather Journal

Date		Sunrise		Sunset	
Sunny	Partly Cloudy	Cloudy	Wind Speed		
Temp Hi	Lo	Humidity		Dewpoint	
Barometric Pressure		Precipitation Amount			
Rain	Sleet	Freezing Rain	Snow	Snow Depth	

Date		Sunrise		Sunset	
Sunny	Partly Cloudy	Cloudy	Wind Speed		
Temp Hi	Lo	Humidity		Dewpoint	
Barometric Pressure		Precipitation Amount			
Rain	Sleet	Freezing Rain	Snow	Snow Depth	

Date		Sunrise		Sunset	
Sunny	Partly Cloudy	Cloudy	Wind Speed		
Temp Hi	Lo	Humidity		Dewpoint	
Barometric Pressure		Precipitation Amount			
Rain	Sleet	Freezing Rain	Snow	Snow Depth	

Weather Journal

Date			Sunrise		Sunset	
Sunny	Partly Cloudy		Cloudy	Wind Speed		
Temp Hi	Lo		Humidity		Dewpoint	
Barometric Pressure			Precipitation Amount			
Rain	Sleet		Freezing Rain	Snow	Snow Depth	

Date			Sunrise		Sunset	
Sunny	Partly Cloudy		Cloudy	Wind Speed		
Temp Hi	Lo		Humidity		Dewpoint	
Barometric Pressure			Precipitation Amount			
Rain	Sleet		Freezing Rain	Snow	Snow Depth	

Date			Sunrise		Sunset	
Sunny	Partly Cloudy		Cloudy	Wind Speed		
Temp Hi	Lo		Humidity		Dewpoint	
Barometric Pressure			Precipitation Amount			
Rain	Sleet		Freezing Rain	Snow	Snow Depth	

Weather Journal

Date		Sunrise		Sunset	
Sunny	Partly Cloudy	Cloudy	Wind Speed		
Temp Hi	Lo	Humidity		Dewpoint	
Barometric Pressure		Precipitation Amount			
Rain	Sleet	Freezing Rain	Snow	Snow Depth	

Date		Sunrise		Sunset	
Sunny	Partly Cloudy	Cloudy	Wind Speed		
Temp Hi	Lo	Humidity		Dewpoint	
Barometric Pressure		Precipitation Amount			
Rain	Sleet	Freezing Rain	Snow	Snow Depth	

Date		Sunrise		Sunset	
Sunny	Partly Cloudy	Cloudy	Wind Speed		
Temp Hi	Lo	Humidity		Dewpoint	
Barometric Pressure		Precipitation Amount			
Rain	Sleet	Freezing Rain	Snow	Snow Depth	

Weather Journal

Date		Sunrise		Sunset	
Sunny	Partly Cloudy	Cloudy	Wind Speed		
Temp Hi Lo		Humidity		Dewpoint	
Barometric Pressure		Precipitation Amount			
Rain	Sleet	Freezing Rain		Snow	Snow Depth

Date		Sunrise		Sunset	
Sunny	Partly Cloudy	Cloudy	Wind Speed		
Temp Hi Lo		Humidity		Dewpoint	
Barometric Pressure		Precipitation Amount			
Rain	Sleet	Freezing Rain		Snow	Snow Depth

Date		Sunrise		Sunset	
Sunny	Partly Cloudy	Cloudy	Wind Speed		
Temp Hi Lo		Humidity		Dewpoint	
Barometric Pressure		Precipitation Amount			
Rain	Sleet	Freezing Rain		Snow	Snow Depth

Weather Journal

Date		Sunrise		Sunset	
Sunny	Partly Cloudy	Cloudy	Wind Speed		
Temp Hi	Lo	Humidity		Dewpoint	
Barometric Pressure		Precipitation Amount			
Rain	Sleet	Freezing Rain	Snow	Snow Depth	

Date		Sunrise		Sunset	
Sunny	Partly Cloudy	Cloudy	Wind Speed		
Temp Hi	Lo	Humidity		Dewpoint	
Barometric Pressure		Precipitation Amount			
Rain	Sleet	Freezing Rain	Snow	Snow Depth	

Date		Sunrise		Sunset	
Sunny	Partly Cloudy	Cloudy	Wind Speed		
Temp Hi	Lo	Humidity		Dewpoint	
Barometric Pressure		Precipitation Amount			
Rain	Sleet	Freezing Rain	Snow	Snow Depth	

Weather Journal

Date			Sunrise		Sunset	
Sunny	Partly Cloudy		Cloudy	Wind Speed		
Temp Hi	Lo		Humidity		Dewpoint	
Barometric Pressure			Precipitation Amount			
Rain	Sleet		Freezing Rain	Snow	Snow Depth	

Date			Sunrise		Sunset	
Sunny	Partly Cloudy		Cloudy	Wind Speed		
Temp Hi	Lo		Humidity		Dewpoint	
Barometric Pressure			Precipitation Amount			
Rain	Sleet		Freezing Rain	Snow	Snow Depth	

Date			Sunrise		Sunset	
Sunny	Partly Cloudy		Cloudy	Wind Speed		
Temp Hi	Lo		Humidity		Dewpoint	
Barometric Pressure			Precipitation Amount			
Rain	Sleet		Freezing Rain	Snow	Snow Depth	

Weather Journal

Date		Sunrise		Sunset	
Sunny	Partly Cloudy	Cloudy	Wind Speed		
Temp Hi Lo		Humidity		Dewpoint	
Barometric Pressure		Precipitation Amount			
Rain	Sleet	Freezing Rain	Snow	Snow Depth	

Date		Sunrise		Sunset	
Sunny	Partly Cloudy	Cloudy	Wind Speed		
Temp Hi Lo		Humidity		Dewpoint	
Barometric Pressure		Precipitation Amount			
Rain	Sleet	Freezing Rain	Snow	Snow Depth	

Date		Sunrise		Sunset	
Sunny	Partly Cloudy	Cloudy	Wind Speed		
Temp Hi Lo		Humidity		Dewpoint	
Barometric Pressure		Precipitation Amount			
Rain	Sleet	Freezing Rain	Snow	Snow Depth	

Weather Journal

Date		Sunrise		Sunset	
Sunny	Partly Cloudy	Cloudy	Wind Speed		
Temp Hi	Lo	Humidity		Dewpoint	
Barometric Pressure		Precipitation Amount			
Rain	Sleet	Freezing Rain	Snow	Snow Depth	

Date		Sunrise		Sunset	
Sunny	Partly Cloudy	Cloudy	Wind Speed		
Temp Hi	Lo	Humidity		Dewpoint	
Barometric Pressure		Precipitation Amount			
Rain	Sleet	Freezing Rain	Snow	Snow Depth	

Date		Sunrise		Sunset	
Sunny	Partly Cloudy	Cloudy	Wind Speed		
Temp Hi	Lo	Humidity		Dewpoint	
Barometric Pressure		Precipitation Amount			
Rain	Sleet	Freezing Rain	Snow	Snow Depth	

Weather Journal

Date		Sunrise		Sunset	
Sunny	Partly Cloudy	Cloudy	Wind Speed		
Temp Hi	Lo	Humidity		Dewpoint	
Barometric Pressure		Precipitation Amount			
Rain	Sleet	Freezing Rain	Snow	Snow Depth	

Date		Sunrise		Sunset	
Sunny	Partly Cloudy	Cloudy	Wind Speed		
Temp Hi	Lo	Humidity		Dewpoint	
Barometric Pressure		Precipitation Amount			
Rain	Sleet	Freezing Rain	Snow	Snow Depth	

Date		Sunrise		Sunset	
Sunny	Partly Cloudy	Cloudy	Wind Speed		
Temp Hi	Lo	Humidity		Dewpoint	
Barometric Pressure		Precipitation Amount			
Rain	Sleet	Freezing Rain	Snow	Snow Depth	

Weather Journal

Date		Sunrise		Sunset	
Sunny	Partly Cloudy	Cloudy	Wind Speed		
Temp Hi	Lo	Humidity		Dewpoint	
Barometric Pressure		Precipitation Amount			
Rain	Sleet	Freezing Rain	Snow	Snow Depth	

Date		Sunrise		Sunset	
Sunny	Partly Cloudy	Cloudy	Wind Speed		
Temp Hi	Lo	Humidity		Dewpoint	
Barometric Pressure		Precipitation Amount			
Rain	Sleet	Freezing Rain	Snow	Snow Depth	

Date		Sunrise		Sunset	
Sunny	Partly Cloudy	Cloudy	Wind Speed		
Temp Hi	Lo	Humidity		Dewpoint	
Barometric Pressure		Precipitation Amount			
Rain	Sleet	Freezing Rain	Snow	Snow Depth	

Weather Journal

Date		Sunrise		Sunset	
Sunny	Partly Cloudy	Cloudy	Wind Speed		
Temp Hi Lo		Humidity		Dewpoint	
Barometric Pressure		Precipitation Amount			
Rain	Sleet	Freezing Rain	Snow	Snow Depth	

Date		Sunrise		Sunset	
Sunny	Partly Cloudy	Cloudy	Wind Speed		
Temp Hi Lo		Humidity		Dewpoint	
Barometric Pressure		Precipitation Amount			
Rain	Sleet	Freezing Rain	Snow	Snow Depth	

Date		Sunrise		Sunset	
Sunny	Partly Cloudy	Cloudy	Wind Speed		
Temp Hi Lo		Humidity		Dewpoint	
Barometric Pressure		Precipitation Amount			
Rain	Sleet	Freezing Rain	Snow	Snow Depth	

Weather Journal

Date		Sunrise		Sunset	
Sunny	Partly Cloudy	Cloudy	Wind Speed		
Temp Hi	Lo	Humidity		Dewpoint	
Barometric Pressure		Precipitation Amount			
Rain	Sleet	Freezing Rain	Snow	Snow Depth	

Date		Sunrise		Sunset	
Sunny	Partly Cloudy	Cloudy	Wind Speed		
Temp Hi	Lo	Humidity		Dewpoint	
Barometric Pressure		Precipitation Amount			
Rain	Sleet	Freezing Rain	Snow	Snow Depth	

Date		Sunrise		Sunset	
Sunny	Partly Cloudy	Cloudy	Wind Speed		
Temp Hi	Lo	Humidity		Dewpoint	
Barometric Pressure		Precipitation Amount			
Rain	Sleet	Freezing Rain	Snow	Snow Depth	

Weather Journal

Totals for the Month of

Sunrise at start of the month	Sunrise at the end of the month
Sunset at start of the month	Sunset at the end of the month
Average high temp	Average low temp
Total precipitation	

Total sunny days	Total partly cloudy days	Total cloud days

Snow depth start of the month	Snow depth end of the month

Totals for the Month of

Sunrise at start of the month	Sunrise at the end of the month
Sunset at start of the month	Sunset at the end of the month
Average high temp	Average low temp
Total precipitation	

Total sunny days	Total partly cloudy days	Total cloud days

Snow depth start of the month	Snow depth end of the month

Weather Journal

Totals for the Month of

Sunrise at start of the month		Sunrise at the end of the month	
Sunset at start of the month		Sunset at the end of the month	
Average high temp		Average low temp	
Total precipitation			
Total sunny days	Total partly cloudy days	Total cloud days	
Snow depth start of the month		Snow depth end of the month	

Totals for the Month of

Sunrise at start of the month		Sunrise at the end of the month	
Sunset at start of the month		Sunset at the end of the month	
Average high temp		Average low temp	
Total precipitation			
Total sunny days	Total partly cloudy days	Total cloud days	
Snow depth start of the month		Snow depth end of the month	

Weather Journal

Totals for the Month of

Sunrise at start of the month	Sunrise at the end of the month	
Sunset at start of the month	Sunset at the end of the month	
Average high temp	Average low temp	
Total precipitation		
Total sunny days	Total partly cloudy days	Total cloud days
Snow depth start of the month	Snow depth end of the month	

Totals for the Month of

Sunrise at start of the month	Sunrise at the end of the month	
Sunset at start of the month	Sunset at the end of the month	
Average high temp	Average low temp	
Total precipitation		
Total sunny days	Total partly cloudy days	Total cloud days
Snow depth start of the month	Snow depth end of the month	

Weather Journal

Totals for the Month of

Sunrise at start of the month		Sunrise at the end of the month	
Sunset at start of the month		Sunset at the end of the month	
Average high temp		Average low temp	
Total precipitation			
Total sunny days	Total partly cloudy days	Total cloud days	
Snow depth start of the month		Snow depth end of the month	

Totals for the Month of

Sunrise at start of the month		Sunrise at the end of the month	
Sunset at start of the month		Sunset at the end of the month	
Average high temp		Average low temp	
Total precipitation			
Total sunny days	Total partly cloudy days	Total cloud days	
Snow depth start of the month		Snow depth end of the month	

Weather Journal

Totals for the Month of

Sunrise at start of the month		Sunrise at the end of the month	
Sunset at start of the month		Sunset at the end of the month	
Average high temp		Average low temp	
Total precipitation			
Total sunny days	Total partly cloudy days		Total cloud days
Snow depth start of the month		Snow depth end of the month	

Totals for the Month of

Sunrise at start of the month		Sunrise at the end of the month	
Sunset at start of the month		Sunset at the end of the month	
Average high temp		Average low temp	
Total precipitation			
Total sunny days	Total partly cloudy days		Total cloud days
Snow depth start of the month		Snow depth end of the month	

Weather Journal

Totals for the Month of

Sunrise at start of the month		Sunrise at the end of the month	
Sunset at start of the month		Sunset at the end of the month	
Average high temp		Average low temp	
Total precipitation			
Total sunny days	Total partly cloudy days	Total cloud days	
Snow depth start of the month		Snow depth end of the month	

Totals for the Month of

Sunrise at start of the month		Sunrise at the end of the month	
Sunset at start of the month		Sunset at the end of the month	
Average high temp		Average low temp	
Total precipitation			
Total sunny days	Total partly cloudy days	Total cloud days	
Snow depth start of the month		Snow depth end of the month	

Made in United States
Orlando, FL
09 May 2025